DISABILITY

DISABILITY
From Social Problem to Federal Program

Irving Howards
Henry P. Brehm
Saad Z. Nagi

PRAEGER

PRAEGER SPECIAL STUDIES • PRAEGER SCIENTIFIC

Library of Congress Cataloging in Publication Data

Howards, Irving.
    Disability, from social problem to federal program.

    Bibliography: p.
    Includes index.
    1. Federal aid to handicapped services--United
States. 2. Handicapped--United States--Socioeconomic
status. I. Brehm, Henry P., joint author. II. Nagi,
Saad Zaghloul, joint author. III. Title.
HV3001.A4H68   362.4'0973   78-19788
ISBN 0-03-046311-4

Published in 1980 by Praeger Publishers
CBS Educational and Professional Publishing
A Division of CBS, Inc.
521 Fifth Avenue, New York, New York 10017 U.S.A.

© 1980 by Praeger Publishers

0123456789   038   987654321

Printed in the United States of America

to our wives

FRIEDA
MOLLY
KAY

PREFACE

In reviewing public policy relative to a series of social insurance and social welfare issues, the authors of this book, in cooperation with other investigators, have used a particular analytic model. A separate presentation will summarize the use of this approach for analyzing the issues in meeting the economic needs of the disabled and widowed through Social Security and in financing the medical care needs of the aged under Medicare.

The present volume discusses in detail the broader issues involved in meeting the needs of the disabled.* It is one of a set of books each of which deals with one of the above-mentioned areas separately but using the same framework. They assess the consistency of focus in the movement from a social problem's conception and identification through formulation of a policy to deal with it and finally to development and implementation of an action program. These books review the results of three Social Security Administration-funded studies with social policy implications. Each study concerns a different population category defined as in need of governmental action to ameliorate the impact of a social problem. In each case, a general policy for solving the problem has been translated into a legislated program. However, there is not necessarily an adequate fit between general policy and the program designed to fulfill that policy. Neither does the policy necessarily indicate an accurate understanding and assessment of the underlying social problem.

In each of the three cases, two primary issues of policy analysis are considered. First, is the general policy, conceptualized explicitly or implicitly for dealing with a specific area of social problem, consonant with or a mismatch to the parameters of the underlying social problem, and does it reflect an adequate conception of the nature and root causes of that problem and an accurate assessment of its scope and dimensions? Second, is there a fit between the policy and the social program, that is, does the formally instituted program usually legislated by government action, with implementing procedures and administrative rules

---

*Portions of this presentation are based on Irving Howards and Henry P. Brehm, *The Ecology of Disability: Analysis of State Population and SSDI Program Administration Characteristics As They Relate to State Rates of Disability*. Final Report SSA Contract No. 71-3380, February 1977.

established by the responsible agency, accomplish the generally stated objectives in dealing with the underlying social problem?

Inconsistency or mismatch within these areas of concern may result in a lack of "success" for the implementation of a social program independent of the level of funding or the operating efficiency in program administration. No attempt is made to assess program administration efficiency as such. The orientation is to the policy's formulation and implementation, and the program's outcome.

The possible reasons for mismatch at the levels of general policy and its view of the problem or of the legislated program designed to accomplish the goals of the policy are discussed to the extent these can be surmised. Some possible "whys" include: a lack of appropriate data on the nature or dimensions of the problem or on what actions might affect it and how; the resolution of opposing social philosophies on approaches toward or responsibilities for social problems; and political compromise negotiated between or for vested interest groups with varying degrees of power.

The analytic framework of problem, policy, and program is used here in dealing with three social problem areas: the economic needs of the widowed, the economic needs of the disabled, and the medical care needs of the aged. The policies for dealing with these social problems are public income maintenance for the widowed and the disabled, and medical care financing for the aged. The three specific programs under consideration are Social Security Survivors Insurance and Disability Insurance and Health Insurance for the Aged (Medicare).

The contention is that some of the difficulties encountered in dealing with the three problem areas may be based on a mismatch at either or both of the levels discussed. If such a mismatch exists, the result of the program might be contrary to the intent of the general policy approach designed to deal with the social problem.

If this happens and the difficulty is not properly identified, proposed solutions may be inappropriate. For example, if data indicate that a given program appropriately matches the policy formulated and that lack of program "success" is due to the policy itself not reflecting a clear understanding of the underlying social problem, then strengthening the administration of the program will not be effective, nor will supplying additional funds for program implementation or making minor changes in the legislative structure of the program or its implementing procedures and administration regulations. It would be necessary to review at the appropriate level what a new policy should be and to redesign the legislated program and its implementation to deal with the underlying social problem as redefined or reassessed.

The three studies that provide the major inputs for these individual volumes perform analyses using data from three distinct methodological approaches. The analytic model is addressed to independent although potentially overlapping areas of social problems.

The analysis for the disability study to be discussed in detail in this volume was based on 1970 U.S. Census of Population data and Social Security Disability Insurance program data on application for and award of benefits and State Disability Determination Services (DDS) characteristics. Differences among states in the rates of self-defined disability and application for and award of benefits under the Social Security Disability Insurance program were analyzed as these related to state economic and social conditions. The administrative characteristics of state DDSs were analyzed as these related to the rates of award.

The background and developmental history to the present legislation authorizing the Social Security Disability Insurance program is reviewed and the social problem toward which the underlying policy was aimed is described. The findings clearly indicate that the policy was aimed at a medical conception of the problem of disability. However, the evidence presented here suggests that the self-definition of disability in the population and, hence, the tendency to apply for disability benefits are based in large measure on individuals' capacity actually to get and hold jobs. It appears that the number of people who define themselves as disabled and, therefore, take action based on that definition may be highly related to social and economic circumstances. These issues and their implications for disability policy and program will be considered in the chapters that follow.

For the study on medical care for the aged, household surveys and community medical facilities surveys were conducted. Comparable cross-sectional data were collected at three points in time: immediately after the passage of Medicare retrospectively for the period prior to its implementation, two years after its implementation, and again two years later. The analysis reported in the companion volume, *Medical Care for the Aged* (Praeger, 1980 publication date), relates primarily to data from a major Midwestern metropolitan area. One conclusion drawn in this analysis is that the policy of providing the aged with greater access to medical care through relief from the pressures of financing this care fits only a limited perspective on the underlying social problem, that is, the need of the aged for assistance in financing health care under circumstances of decreased economic means.

However, a second conclusion is that the policy and program do not satisfy the unique health care needs of the aged because the program does not alter the working relationships, organizational structure, planning, coordination, or decision-making apparatus of the system for delivering medical care to the U.S. population in general and the aged in particular. The result is that the present medical care delivery system has effectively co-opted the financial mechanism established under Medicare. While theoretically the aged are less responsible for financing their own medical care, there is concern for the amount of out-of-pocket cost they are still paying and also serious doubt as to whether there has been any significant realignment among the providers of medical care to provide more appropriate services for the aged.

For the study of widowhood, there was a household survey of current and recent past beneficiaries, with a small sampling of widows who had received only a lump sum burial benefit. The interview asked about the various support systems available to and used by the widow for her economic, social, and emotional support. The companion volume, *Widowhood* (Praeger, 1980 publication date), deals with the widow's economic support and its relationship to her current life-cycle situation.

Policy in the area of benefits for the widowed population seems not to have recognized the full extent of two aspects of the problem of widowhood. First, widows who are either caring for minor children or are themselves of relatively advanced age are not the only widows in need of assistance. Also, the possibility that the present generation of widows has characteristics unlike those of generations of widows to follow has not been taken into consideration in formulating a policy and implementing a program. The present generation of widows includes a higher percentage either born outside the United States or married to men born outside the United States than is anticipated for future generations of widows. As a result, these widows and/or their husbands often received only minimal education. Many of these women did not work under the social security system themselves and had husbands who earned relatively low levels of benefits under the system. The enactment of a program to care for the needs of a generation of widows including many such women would not necessarily be appropriate for a generation of widows more of whom were born in the United States, received higher levels of education, and married men with more education than their predecessors. The husbands of such women had better jobs and were entitled to higher retirement benefits, and their widows were entitled to higher benefits as survivors. Also, these widows were more likely to work under the system and earn benefits in their own right.

The size of the female U.S. population who were widows around the time of the study is indicated by reference to the 1970 census. The highest percentage of beneficiary widows are 60 years of age and over, the age at which they can receive benefits based on age. The women in the study who are younger than age 60 are either mothers of minor children who are receiving benefits based on the age of their children, ex-beneficiaries whose children are too old to permit the payment of benefits based on the care of the husband's dependent children or who have remarried, or women who received only lump sum burial benefits.

An omission in the formal program as it relates to the general policy of caring for widows is any form of transitional coverage or other assistance for the widow whose youngest child has reached majority but who is not old enough herself to receive benefits based on age. This group is totally omitted from the social security program despite the existence of a social problem. For these women there is no Social Security Administration (SSA) program to help them re-enter the job market or otherwise reorganize their lives.

It is understandable that no direct benefit would be paid to a widow in her early 50s who was not disabled. However, many women in that age group have left the job market, and while many are potentially capable of reentry not all are currently equipped to do so. By concentrating primarily on the needs of the young widow with minor children, many of whom also could be helped reenter the job market and also may soon reach the transitional period, and the needs of the older widow who represents a unique generation which may be passing out of existence, we have ignored the needs of the widow in-between, whom for practical purposes we have defined as a non-widow.

This is the thrust of this set of books. It is our hope they will contribute to the literature on policy formulation and program planning as related to the handling of social problems and also to a better understanding of the issues in each of the specific areas of concern.

CONTENTS

PREFACE   vi

LIST OF TABLES AND FIGURES   xii

Chapter

1   SOCIAL PROBLEM, SOCIAL POLICY, AND SOCIAL PROGRAM   1

2   STATEMENT OF THE PROBLEM   31

3   THE ESTABLISHMENT OF DISABILITY INSURANCE: POLICY
    FORMULATION AND PROGRAM DEVELOPMENT   50

4   THE RELATIONSHIP BETWEEN DISABILITY AND
    SOCIOECONOMIC CONDITIONS   68

5   THE ADMINISTRATION OF DISABILITY DETERMINATION AND
    FEDERAL-STATE RELATIONSHIPS   88

6   CONCLUSIONS AND IMPLICATIONS   110

REFERENCES   133

Appendix

A: LIST OF STUDY VARIABLES   139

B: DATA INPUT FOR EACH STUDY VARIABLE BY STATE   143

C: MULTIPLE REGRESSIONS, U.S. CENSUS OF POPULATION, 1970:
    DISAGGREGATED DISABILITY MEASURES (SELF-DEFINED)
    AND SOCIOECONOMIC CHARACTERISTICS   153

INDEX   168

ABOUT THE AUTHORS   172

LIST OF TABLES AND FIGURES

Table   Page

2.1 Rates of Work Disability Reported in the Social Security
       Administration's Survey of Disabled Adults   37

2.2 Work Disability and Other Characteristics of Respondents
       18-64 Years of Age   40

2.3 Percent Distribution of Persons with Limitation of Activity,
       by Selected Chronic Conditions Causing Limitation,
       According to Degree of Limitation, United States, 1974   42

2.4 Severity of Disability, by Major Disabling Condition,
       Percentage Distribution of Disabled Adults Aged 18-64,
       by Severity of Disability, Spring 1966   44

2.5 Responses to Items Comprising Physical and Emotional
       Performance Scales   46

2.6 The Relations of Limitations in Function and Work Disability   47

4.1 Stepwise Multiple Regression State Self-Defined Disability
       Rate and Socioeconomic Characteristics   71

4.2 Stepwise Multiple Regression State Self-Defined Severe
       Disability Rate and Socioeconomic Characteristics   72

4.3 Stepwise Multiple Regression State Self-Defined Partial
       Disability Rate and Socioeconomic Characteristics   73

4.4 Stepwise Multiple Regression SSDI Application (Initial
       Determination) Rate per Disability-Insured Population
       and Socioeconomic Characteristics   79

4.5 Awards per 100,000 Disability-Insured Population, 1970   83

4.6 Applications per 100,000 Disability-Insured Population, 1970   83

5.1 Correlations between Application (Initial Allowance) Rates
       per Disability-Insured Population and Twelve DDS
       Administrative Professionalism Variables   105

Table   Page

5.2 Award (Allowance) Rate per Disability-Insured Population and
        DDS Administrative Professionalism Variables   107

Figure

5.1 Guidelines for Identifying the Range of Residual
        Functional Capacity   91

5.2 Sequential Evaluation   93

5.3 Percentage of Total Allowances and Denials, Excluding
        Technical Denials, San Francisco Region, 1970   95

5.4 Guidelines for C1-1502(b) Cases   98

DISABILITY

1
SOCIAL PROBLEM, SOCIAL POLICY, AND SOCIAL PROGRAM

Understanding social welfare policy in the United States is a frightening task given the size of social welfare expenditures, its almost exponential growth, and the plethora of welfare programs in need of analysis. Cash benefits alone increased from $4 billion in 1940, to over $150 billion in 1976. They are expected to be $200 billion by 1980. Total social welfare expenditures, including those of voluntary agencies, constituted 25 percent of the 1971 gross national product (GNP) (Macarov 1978).

These expenditures are a reflection of the tremendous proliferation of social welfare programs. Since the passage of the Social Security Act in 1935, so many new programs have been established and new agencies created to administer them that a diagram of the Department of Health, Education, and Welfare reflecting the relationships of administrative units responsible for social welfare resembles "a wiring diagram for a new type of space capsule" (Macarov 1978). Such a diagram does not even take into account the equally complicated administrative arrangements in state and local governments with social welfare responsibilities. Nor does it reflect the fact that in 1975 there were approximately 6 million voluntary organizations in the United States providing some sort of health and welfare services (Macarov 1978).

Focusing on different categories of social welfare does not particularly expedite comprehension. If the interest is in ways of meeting the economic needs of the aged, the focus could be on retirement or survivors' insurance benefits under Social Security or on Supplemental Security Income (SSI) for the

1

aged. Both these programs provide financial benefits for the aged, but on different philosophical and practical bases. If the interest is in the financing of medical care costs, attention could be directed toward Medicare or Medicaid. The same distinctions exist between these programs as between Old Age and Survivors Insurance (OASI) and SSI, with the implications these distinctions suggest for policy, populations covered, and the general operation of the programs.

A similar difficulty exists in attempting to understand the programs presumably designed to meet the problem of poverty in general since the issues of aging and poverty obviously overlap. The relationship between social insurance and public assistance and its economic and political implications for poverty program development could be reviewed. The development of public assistance in this country before and since the Social Security Act of 1935 and the original provisions in that act, which provided federal and state funds for the aged, could be examined. This examination would include the movement from a federal-state matching funds program of assistance for the aged poor administered by the states to the national program providing a minimum guaranteed income under SSI in 1974. However, poverty among the non-aged has been handled separately. Cash assistance to families with dependent children could be examined from its inception in 1935 (ADC) through its various changes in emphasis and coverage, including the provision in some states for aid to families with an unemployed parent (AFDC-UP) and subsidization of day-care centers for the children of mothers with dependent children. Housing programs, with all of their ramifications for different population groups in our society, could be analyzed. Food stamps could be viewed from the perspective of the program's original purpose (to alleviate farm surplus) to its present objective, that is, to provide adequate and nutritional food for those in need. The War on Poverty programs could be investigated to see what they offered to alleviate poverty in the 1960s and how successful they have been (for example, see Haveman 1977, especially chapter 2).

Trying to understand how the problems of disability have been met leads to the same confusion of multiplicity. Programs for the disabled run the gamut from insurance benefits for those unable to work before usual retirement age and the provision of a guaranteed income to those disabled who qualify under the SSI program, to service-oriented activities, including those concentrating on rehabilitation and employment. There are programs which relate only to special population groups, such as veterans. A recent study on disability observed that by 1973 the federal government had spent $40 billion, or 3 percent of its GNP, on 64 separate disability programs (Berkowitz 1976, p. 1).

As might be expected, these programs vary in purpose and scope. They include such different approaches as efforts to provide subsidized housing and accessible public facilities for the disabled and workers' compensation against loss of income, medical expenses, or death due to work-related injuries or illness. About 85 percent of all employees are covered under this program with benefits reaching $6.7 billion (Consulting Group on Welfare Reform 1977). The compensation program for veterans, their dependents, and survivors for service-connected disability or death provides benefits to 3.5 million recipients (2.3 million veterans and 1.2 million dependents and survivors) (Consulting Group on Welfare Reform 1977). The Railway Retirement, Disability and Survivors Insurance program provides $3.6 billion to 1 million beneficiaries. Disability benefits are paid for permanent and total disability if the employee has completed at least ten years of service, and for a disability for the regular job after at least 20 years of service (Consulting Group on Welfare Reform 1977). Coal miners receive benefits if they become totally disabled as a result of work-related pneumoconiosis (black lung). A miner's widow, orphan, dependent parent, brother, or sister are also entitled to benefits if death occurred because of the disease. Vocational rehabilitation is provided to individuals with mental and physical handicaps to encourage them to work despite their impairments. The estimated 1977 cost was approximately $900 million; the estimated number of recipients 1.8 million.

The SSI program is designed to provide a basic guaranteed income for needy disabled and blind, as well as the aged. Before the disabled receive benefits they must establish financial need as defined by the program and must meet the same specifications as those under the Social Security Disability Insurance program for determining disability. For fiscal year 1977, it was estimated that the SSI program would cost $6.3 billion ($4.7 billion representing the federal contribution) and reach 4.4 million beneficiaries, of whom 2.2 million were blind or disabled (Consulting Group on Welfare Reform 1977). The SSI program also contains a Services to Disabled Children component, whereby blind or disabled children under 16 receive benefits and are the focus of rehabilitation efforts. This aspect of the SSI program has a $30 million federal ceiling and is designed to provide benefits for an estimated 16,000 children annually (Consulting Group on Welfare Reform 1977).

Finally, the national program of disability insurance under Social Security, which is the specific program of interest in this book, provides benefits for those who are unable to engage in "substantial gainful activity" because their health impairments are so severe. A claimant must have worked a sufficient number of quarters in covered employment in the period preceding application to be insured for disability benefits. The estimated 1977 cost for the program's benefits was $10.9 billion (Consulting Group on Welfare Reform 1977).

It should be apparent that understanding social welfare policy and programs is immensely difficult given the proliferation, complexity, and apparent conflicts and overlaps in purpose and orientation that exist in this area. Approaching the analysis of public social welfare policy in view of the array of programs requires a framework to reduce this confusion. What is necessary is a vehicle for analyzing public policy which focuses on the underlying concern of all such programs, that is, whether they are alleviating the social problems for which they presumably were designed and what difference the program actually makes to those directly affected by the social problem. It is with this goal in mind that we are using an analytic technique which concentrates upon how social problems are defined, how policies are related to these definitions, how programs reflect the policies, and how this entire process affects the problem population. This analytic approach, as briefly reviewed in the Preface to this volume, attempts to assess a public policy and the program designed to foster it with a primary focus on the underlying problem as it was and might have been defined as the basis for concern and societal action. Integrating the three dimensions of concern in an area — the problem, the policy, and the program — into one analytical framework provides a vehicle for dealing jointly with the issues within a given area.

This mode of analysis suggests that social problems, social policies, and social programs should be interrelated. How a social problem is defined suggests the extent to which society assumes an obligation for the amelioration of the problem through social policy. A social program is then enacted to implement the goals and objectives of the social policy formulated. Since the ultimate result of this process is supposed to be a congruence between the original problem and the policy and program designed to deal with it, relief should be provided for the target population defined as affected by the social problem. However, if the original definition of the social problem is, to some extent, inaccurate, the situation may not be relieved.

Recognition of these interrelationships expedites understanding of public policy since it encourages the observer to focus on key concerns, for example, the factors which influence the definition of a social problem and how; the extent to which public policy is actually a derivative of a problem's definition; whether the program developed implements policy goals and objectives; whether implementation of the program provides relief for the population affected by the problem; and, given the nature of the underlying problem, whether that relief is meaningful.

The ability to analyze public policy by using this approach depends upon understanding the essence of social problems, their definition, the policies and programs for dealing with them, and the factors that contribute to the form these policies and programs take. Throughout this presentation we will be assessing how society's definition of a social problem relates to data on its nature; whether public policy matches or is at odds with the problem as it was defined or as it might have been defined given the available data; and whether a social program does indeed match the social policy it was to implement. Understanding social problem definition is key to assessing social welfare policy and its impact. Social values are of prime importance in how a problem is defined and in the general direction taken by social policies and programs.

This chapter's major purpose is to review how we approach analyzing the area of attempting to alleviate disability's effects by providing cash benefits for workers under Social Security. We are interested in determining the impact of dealing with disability as it has been viewed by the program given an apparently valid alternate approach, that people with health impairments may have an increased potential for being considered disabled and unable to work because of limitations of the job market in its general availability of employment opportunities. The subleties of this distinction will be clarified in later discussion. In the remainder of this book we will concentrate upon how disability has been defined, the factors which seem to have influenced this definition, and how this has been reflected in the legislative process and program specifics. We will also review the impact of the administrative structure in which decision makers function on who receives benefits. As a concluding issue, we will assess the disability insurance program from the perspective of whether the policy it has implemented has been an appropriate way to deal with the problem of disability and then review some possible alternatives.

Social Problems, Policies, and Programs – Some Definitions

Before we proceed with a discussion of the issues in disability the terms social problem, policy, and programs as we use them must be clarified.

We have defined problem as a situation or condition which negatively affects a significant portion of the population and needs a solution through collective action. By this definition we mean that a problem is the collective result of a pattern of behavior or circumstance which does not conform to social expectation or which impedes social performance (Ryan 1976, p. 13). People with limited incomes may be unable to afford adequate housing, medical care, food, clothing, and so on. Older persons frequently live on reduced incomes because they have retired or their health makes them unable to work. At this time of their lives they are in increasing need of expensive medical care. The disabled may find that their health limits their ability to perform or function as others in society. In industrial societies whose citizens are expected to be productive workers these conditions are viewed as a problem.

A social policy is established when society assumes some degree of obligation for the relief of a social problem. Policy, as we use the term, is a set of general statements of objectives embodied implicitly and/or explicitly in legislation that addresses the problem. Social policies, therefore, contain the goals in alleviating social problems. Public social welfare policy is a course of action adopted by the government "having a direct impact on the welfare of the citizens by providing them with services and incomes." (T. H. Marshall, as quoted in Morris 1979, p. 2; Titmuss 1974, p. 23).

Since a social policy is designed to alleviate a societal problem, it is associated with how society has defined the problem. The ramifications of how the problem is defined will be explored in some detail later. However, it is important to consider this association briefly here so that the intimacy of the relationship can be appreciated. For example, if the indigent elderly are defined as poor because of a history of low earnings employment or marginal attachment to the labor force, they may be provided means-tested income supplementation. On the other hand, if the elderly have a reasonable work history and are defined as having problems associated with age which exist through no fault of their own, such as an increased need for medical care and a limited income because of retirement, public policy probably will be more generous.

Where disability is the issue, if society defines the problem as one in which health conditions clearly prevent people from working, public policy may take the form of providing income-maintenance benefits for the permanently and totally disabled. Vocational rehabilitation would be included to promote the social value of return to the work force, if possible. However, the primary emphasis would be on cash benefits. On the other hand, if disability were defined in terms of a combination of limited job market and individual capacity, the policy logically could focus less on ascertaining that a health condition clearly prevents work and more on providing jobs or, alternately, temporary income maintenance until employment becomes available.

A social program is the specific legislative mechanism chosen to accomplish policy goals and objectives. It is the action aspect of policy. Medicaid and Old Age Assistance (after 1974, Supplemental Security Income) are examples of programs designed to carry out the policy intent of helping the indigent aged by a welfare-oriented approach (where eligibility is income or means-tested). Social insurance programs, such as Medicare and Old Age and Survivors' Insurance (OASI), provide benefits for the aged based on their work histories. The policy position is that these benefits are an earned right and that without them the aged would have inadequate economic resources in retirement. Disability Insurance and Vocational Rehabilitation are programs which seek to meet the policy goals of helping those who no longer can work, when disability is defined from the perspective of inability to work because of impaired health and when rehabilitation is seen as a mechanism for returning people to the work force if possible.

FACTORS INFLUENCING HOW SOCIAL
PROBLEMS ARE DEFINED

Values and Social Problems

We have already stressed the importance of knowing how a problem is defined for understanding public policy. The collective beliefs or values society holds regarding its obligations for problem alleviation are crucial to understanding the process of policy formulation. Values are affected by other factors. Indeed, a host of intervening characteristics may affect values and the ultimate direction public policy takes. We will examine some of these in the process of reviewing the importance of a series of factors in the policy formulation process. What we suggest is that the broad configuration of such factors and public policy in general are shaped by social values.

There is considerable support for this position. Max Weber observed that "normative standards of value can and must be the objects of dispute and discussion of a problem of social policy" (Weber 1949, pp. 56-57). Titmuss indicated that there "is no escape from value choices in welfare systems" and that those who are interested in policy analysis "must inevitably be concerned with 'what is and what might be'; with what we (as members of society) want (the ends); and how we get there (the means)" (Titmuss 1974, p. 132). Gunnar Myrdal reminds us, "Things look differently, depending upon 'where you stand.' Prior to answers there must be questions. And there can be no view except from a viewpoint. In the questions raised and the viewpoint applied valuations are implied" (Myrdal 1976).

Rein agrees, noting, "What is needed in social policy is not so much good tools, but good questions" (Rein 1970, p. x). He maintains that a study of social policy must be "above all concerned with choice among competing values" and that consequently it is "sterile" and "misleading" to "pursue techniques of analysis divorced from issues of purpose because techniques arise to serve purposes and therefore imply value assumptions." He therefore suggests that public policy analysis relate "the actual working of social policy to questions of value" (Rein 1974, pp. 62-63).

Reisman observed that "no policy can escape from values, ideologies and images of what constitutes the 'good society' " (Reisman 1977, p. 11). Navarro puts the point rather brusquely when he observes that "all social analysis, however dispassionate or adorned with elegant statistical presentation ... is value-laden ... [and] are ideologies in disguise." (Navarro 1976, p. x). Connally expresses similar sentiments in his discussion of how public interest is determined. He criticizes approaches to policy analysis which focus on juridicial democracy as the means of providing for the public interest. By this he means those who maintain that social problems can be ameliorated if the influence of specialized pressure groups is diminished. Juridicial democrats maintain that this can be accomplished by precisely defining public policy in the law to prevent usurpation of public interest, establishing an independent civil service, and making certain that the process of law making is pushed up from bureaucracies to Congress where issues and debate are more visible (Connally 1977).

The major relevance of value systems to how social welfare problems are defined concerns their focus on the cause of these problems and the responsibility for their alleviation. Views on these two matters are essentially divided between the "collectivists" and the "individualists" (see Connally 1977; George and Wilding 1976). Collectivists tend to feel that most social problems flow from an inherent societal tendency (especially in capitalistic systems) to perpetuate class and income inequalities, limit employment, and restrict access to such "public" services as education, housing, and health care. Since society is considered basically at fault for these conditions it is expected to offer a variety of welfare policies to aid in their alleviation. In Great Britain, for example, policies are designed to provide for "maximum" full employment, a guaranteed income, free health care, and equal educational opportunities (see Furniss and Tilton 1977; George and Wilding 1976). However, there is considerable controversy over whether such policies are truly effective. In Sweden there is a conscious effort to become involved in "preventive measures" (Myrdal, as described in Furniss and Tilton 1977, p. 37) to forestall the occurrence of "social disorders" such as unemployment, urban slums, and illiteracy. Consequently, policies are designed to reduce class and income inequalities, assure a high level of employment, provide for joint labor and management input into wage determination, offer a substantive guaranteed income, and provide free and extensive public services, such as health care, education, and housing.*

As the name implies, individualists take a different view of social problems and societal obligation for their relief. They stress that most social problems can be avoided if people are given the opportunity to exercise their initiative. Given this position, individualists tend to define most social problems as the fault of the individual, that is, as resulting from the absence of individual initiative. The United States is the prime example of a society whose value system stresses that social problems can be avoided if people are left free to exercise their initiative.

A consequence of this assessment of social problems is that governmental policies for social problem alleviation are pursued reluctantly. Indeed, some maintain that the focus upon individualism means that "there are two 'natural' or socially given channels through which an individual's needs are properly met; the private market and the family. Only when these break down should social welfare come into play and then only temporarily." "The true object [they charge] . . . is to teach people how to do without it" (Titmuss 1974, pp. 30-31; Furniss and Tilton 1977, p. 2; Peacock, as quoted in Titmuss 1974, p. 31). Others, although taking a less critical view, agree that individualism means that U.S. social welfare policy "reluctantly" admits more of the needy poor to the relief rolls. (Steiner, as quoted in Furniss and Tilton 1977, p. 180; Piven and Cloward 1970; James 1972: Rimlinger 1971).

In fact, individualists have different views about the degree of responsibility which the individual and/or society should assume for problem alleviation. There are the "anti-collectivists," including F. A. Hayek in England and Milton Friedman in the United States, who argue that "man must be as free as possible to pursue his interests and to bear the consequences of his actions." They agree that most social problems result from individual negligence. On the other hand, "reluctant collectivists" (John Maynard Keynes and John Kenneth Galbraith in the United States, and Wm. C. Beveridge in Great Britain), although agreeing

---

*As in Great Britain, there has been increasing criticism of the Swedish system, with charges that unemployment and inflation are increasing, that class inequalities continue, and that taxes to support such a system of public welfare are excessive (see Furniss and Tilton 1977; also Haveman 1977).

with the anti-collectivists about the importance of individual liberty, feel that there are circumstances when government involvement is necessary in order to alleviate societal problems (George and Wilding 1976, p. 42).* However, they very carefully specify the circumstances under which government should define a problem as requiring governmental intervention (George and Wilding 1976, chapter 3; Galbraith 1967; and Keynes 1926).

The presence of these two views about the nature of social problems in the United States has meant that social problems tend to be defined in terms of the degree of fault to be assigned to the individual and/or society. For instance, some social problems may be defined as resulting from events over which individuals have no control. Wars, aging, a depressed economy, and the death of a husband or father fall into this category (Galbraith 1967). A war may result in an individual's disablement or inability to work or engage in other normal life pursuits. A depressed economy may result in the absence of job opportunities. Aging may mean that once normally productive persons will no longer be able to work. Death may deprive dependents of earnings from the major provider. Since these are events over which the individual presumably has no control, society evaluates the resultant social problems sympathetically. However, a distinction will be made in terms of societal fault for the problem. Veterans' benefits is an ideal example of a program designed to implement policy for a category of social problem defined as entirely society's and not at all the individual's fault.

For Unemployment Insurance the situation is less clear. This program for all practical purposes is administered by the states. Although the federal government establishes a financial minimum and basic eligibility, the amount of benefits and the period during which such benefits may be given vary among states. This may in part represent different views about the degree to which unemployment is society's fault even when it occurs because of a depression.

For some problems, neither society nor the individual can be held responsible. As a result, there are limitations on the amount of societal responsibility assumed for their amelioration as compared to when society is considered the source of the problem. However, these limitations are not as great as those imposed when the social problem is defined as one to which both society and the individual have contributed.

The widows of deceased workers or people with a history of attachment to the labor force who find themselves faced with unanticipated problems, such as disability or the need to make large expenditures for medical care in old age, are examples of persons affected by situations which are neither their fault nor society's. Age-related infirmity increases the need for medical care. Disabled persons may be unable to work because of their health impairments. Widows of

---

*The terms "anti-collectivist" and "reluctant collectivist" are adopted from George and Wilding.

workers have financial problems because of the loss of the major breadwinner. Old Age and Survivors Insurance established by the Social Security Act of 1935 is an example of a program designed to implement policy for this category of social problem. It is designed to provide benefits to previously productive persons (and their dependents) who are in need through no fault of their own. It is financed from payroll taxes paid by employers and employees, administration is federal, and benefits are allocated uniformly for similarly qualified people.

Events over which the individual is considered to have some control are not treated as sympathetically. Assessing responsibility for a social problem on a categorical basis is not easy and different standards and orientations exist. In most instances, the issue is not so much evaluating *when* individuals can be considered to have control over events leading to a social problem as much as assessing the *degree* of control which can be regarded as individual rather than societal.

Poverty may be viewed as a condition to which both society and the individual have contributed. Society may be responsible because it provides limited socioeconomic opportunities to its members. The resultant social problems may be extensive — inadequate housing and education, high rates of unemployment, crime and drug addiction, and generally poor nutrition and medical care (especially for the aged). However, not all with limited socioeconomic opportunities are inadequately housed and educated, unemployed, or criminals or drug addicts. Evidently, then, there is an extent to which affected populations do have control over their status even under such circumstances.

Income-tested policies generally are designed for social problems defined as being caused by both societal and individual negligence. The objective of such policies is to provide nominal financial assistance while encouraging recipients to return to the work force when possible or otherwise to provide for their own support within the family structure.

However, there are varying assessments of the degree of fault which can be assigned to individuals for this category of social problem. This is reflected by varying income-tested program approaches. The SSI program is federally administered and provides a national standard for guaranteed minimum income for the indigent aged, blind, and disabled, recognizing that such people may be less able to help themselves than other poor people. Cash payments for families with dependent children (AFDC) is state-administered, although financing is provided from general revenues of both the federal and state governments. There are state-to-state differences in the program as a result.

Medicare was adopted in line with the policy assumption that the problem of need for medical care and for help in financing such care among the aged is not the fault of the individual or society. Medicare is a form of social insurance; however, the patient is responsible for sharing some of the costs of care. It is interesting to contrast Medicare to Medicaid. The latter was adopted in line with the general policy toward the problems of the poor, where it is assumed that their need for financial assistance results from individual and societal factors contributing to poverty in general. The assistance is more comprehensive but more punitively provided and with a social stigma attached. Consequently, the policy results in payment for medical care through a state-administered, means-tested program financed from general revenues as compared to the earned right, universal, contributory approach of Medicare.

Disability provides an interesting example of the impact of how society defines a social problem and attributes fault or responsibility. As indicated earlier, those disabled as a result of service in the country's wars are accorded the highest consideration, since society assumes total responsibility for their condition. Work-related injuries and illnesses are defined as a result of the employer-controlled work environment and treated accordingly. However, the situation is different for those whose work-limiting health impairments stem from other causes. The disability itself is regarded as the fault of neither society nor the individual. The social problem is defined from two perspectives, the ability to work and the work history of the individual. Disability that is not the result of war or the work setting is defined very carefully as an instance where an impairment is so severe that substantial gainful activity is impossible. The severity of the impairment is evaluated medically in order to have precise and objective criteria for determining whether the impairment is indeed so severe that substantial work is impossible. (We will explore the ramifications of this approach toward determining disability below.) However, if the individual does not have a history of attachment to the labor force, he or she is considered to have contributed to the resultant economic plight and is treated more harshly than would otherwise be the case, in other words, benefits are given only on a means-tested basis and not as social insurance.

The Effect of History on Problem Definition

Values, like most phenomena, may be affected by historical events. Two of the more dramatic illustrations is the influence wars and massive economic dislocations have had upon how society defines social problems and its obligation for their solution.

Before World War II, Great Britain was considered to be at best a variant of a value system in which "individual stress was regarded as a mark of social incapacity" (Titmuss, as quoted in Reisman 1977, p. 12). But when Hitler bombed English cities evacuation of mothers and their children "led to reports of lice, skin diseases, undernourishment, poor clothing, and exposed the extent of bad housing and poverty" (Reisman 1977, p. 12). "The shock to public opinion . . . rivalled the outcry after the Boer War with its disclosures of sickness and low physical standards" (Titmuss, as quoted in Reisman 1977, p. 12). Furthermore a "common purpose" was derived from wartime setbacks suffered by all, such as the bombings and the Dunkerque evacuation. As a result, "the mood of the people changed and, in sympathetic response, values changed as well." (Titmuss, as quoted in Reisman 1977, p. 13). This change in attitudes carried over to post-World War II Britain. World War II was thus immediately responsible for the Beveridge Report of 1942, which outlined a policy of extensive societal responsibility in the areas of health, education, and income support. The Education Act of 1944 and the National Health Service Act of 1948 are programmatic evidence of this change in attitude. As Reisman suggests, "Hitler's bombs succeeded ... in imposing a *de facto* structure of universalism of a multitude of welfare benefits" (Reisman 1977, p. 12).

The Social Security Act of 1935 represents the effects of the "Great Depression" of the early 1930s upon how needs and problems of U.S. society were defined. This was the inevitable result of the fact that by 1933 over 25 percent of the civilian labor force was unemployed and approximately 40 percent of the population in some of the states was on relief. The provision of aid to such numbers of needy was far beyond the fiscal capabilities of state governments, which were responsible for dealing with such problems. Up to this point in U.S. history it had been assumed that if people worked they would be successful. Yet, it was obvious in this instance that many were in difficult circumstances despite the exercise of individual initiative because of the absence of economic opportunities. It was also apparent that the limited economic situation further intensified the problems for those in need because of other reasons.

The Social Security Act attempted to deal with the prevention of poverty and economic insecurity in two ways. The longer-term problem of economic dislocation among the aged was addressed through the approach of social insurance programs financed by payroll taxes paid by employees and employers. The more immediate need for financial aid was addressed through public assistance programs financed from general revenues. Social insurance was represented by the old age benefit program, which eventually became OASI with the addition of survivors insurance in 1939. Disability insurance was added in 1956 and Medicare in 1965. In these programs, benefits are allocated when specified circumstances are met relating to age, disability, death, and so on as a matter of right because of contributions made by the claimants while still working. Public assistance programs were represented by the Aid to Dependent Children program (later AFDC), Aid to the Blind, Aid to the Permanently and Totally Disabled, and Old Age Assistance (which in 1974 were incorporated into the Supplemental Security Income program). Medicaid was added in 1965. In these programs, aid is given according to need regardless of whether the recipient has contributed directly to the program's financial support.

The Nature of Social Problems as an Aspect of Problem Definition

Values suggest the general boundaries for social problem definition, while history provides clues as to how and why attitudes toward and definitions of social problems change. Both are related to society's determination of the nature of a social problem.

Lewis Anthony Dexter, in his book *Tyranny of Schooling*, helps us understand how social problems can be defined from various perspectives. Dexter emphasizes that our social value system stresses that children must attend school and learn and that education is the cornerstone for individual achievement. Compulsory education, therefore, is supported as essential for success in adult life, both for employment and general citizenship. Some measure of educational attainment is a prerequisite for employment even where the connection between the two is not well defined.

Given the emphasis upon compulsory education and learning, schooling is made an ordeal for children who cannot effectively absorb an education through no fault of their own, for example, the borderline mentally retarded child. They are unable to conform with a formula which maintains that existence in society can be eased by education and education can be encouraged by making it compulsory. However, if the mentally retarded do not constitute a difficulty for society in other ways, and Dexter suggests that they do not, then mental retardation may be a social problem only because of the requirement for universal compulsory childhood education. Under these circumstances, we might consider compulsory education as the problem rather than mental retardation. However, to do so runs contrary to a view which is thoroughly ingrained in our child-rearing practices, our legal structure, and our educational standards for employment. It runs contrary to all our preconceptions and social values. In short, how we determine the nature of a social problem is based on our own preset notions.

The way in which the nature of the problem is conceived and defined is important to the policy chosen for problem alleviation. For example, in both the United States and Great Britain, black lung disease is considered a social problem. However, there are significant differences in how it is viewed. In the United States, the problem is defined from the perspective of those who have the disease and its effect on their work capacity and life expectancy. Consequently, disability and survivors benefits are provided. In Great Britain, the problem is defined from the perspective of the conditions of the coal mines themselves. As a result, legislation exists requiring that coal mines be washed down in order to prevent coal dust from affecting the miners.

How the nature of a social problem is defined is associated also with how seriously it is viewed and how responsibility or fault is allocated. This affects whether and what social policy is offered for problem amelioration. There is not always agreement among elements of society on these definitions. A current example is the use of marijuana. There are those in our society who maintain that its possession is not a major problem, since in their view marijuana use is relatively harmless. Consequently, they view the problem in terms of societal intervention in the matter and press for its legalization. Others argue that since marijuana use is dangerous to one's health, laws against its possession and use should be enforced. Interestingly, both sides on this issue use their evaluation about the seriousness of cigarette and liquor consumption to support their positions. Advocates of marijuana suggest that cigarette and liquor consumption constitute a far greater social problem than marijuana use; opponents maintain that cigarette and liquor use is not as serious a social problem as marijuana consumption.

The matter of how seriously different groups in society view a problem also has implications for more traditional areas of concern. For example, debate over the establishment of National Health Insurance centers in part on disagreement over whether personal health in the United States suffers because of the inability to afford medical care and gain access to skilled medical facilities. Some argue that the state of health in the United States is good and that this is the result of expenditures constituting about 10 percent of our GNP. The public programs of Medicare and Medicaid and private health insurance coverage facilitate use of care services. Others maintain that the problem of health care remains a serious social issue despite these programs and the large expenditures (Fuchs 1974; and Morris 1979, chapter 4). Similar disagreements exist regarding the nature and, therefore, the seriousness of almost any social problem in the United States.

FACTORS INFLUENCING SOCIAL POLICY

As we have indicated, the purpose of social policy is to alleviate an existing problem. The extent to which this can be accomplished depends in part upon how the problem is defined, what aspects of it the policy addresses, the resources available for problem amelioration, and the existence of competing problems or policies. How the nature of a problem is defined suggests much about public policy.

Defining the problem of health as centering on the difficulties in utilizing needed and appropriate health care because of affordability suggests it can be dealt with by improving people's ability to pay for sophisticated medical facilities. Focusing on a different aspect of the health problem of the population could result in preventive policies emphasizing the need to change these environmental conditions which may contribute to poor health. An alternate policy approach to the problem viewed as the need for care delivery could focus on directly providing people with inexpensive paramedical aid as well as more sophisticated help when necessary and making medical facilities accessible by placing them by neighborhoods or regions.*

*It was this type of policy approach which resulted in the establishment of Neighborhood Health Centers as one of the War on Poverty programs. Although 1,000 such facilities were planned, only 100 are now in existence. (See Karen Davis, "Policy Development in Health Care," pp. 214-20, in Haveman 1977).

The War on Poverty was "premised" on the view that the problem of poverty was low market productivity. "The poor were viewed as being in that state because they did not work enough or because their manager skills and qualifications were insufficient to raise them out of poverty even if they did work hard." The "remedy" decided on was to "improve the performance of the economy, the productivity of the poor, and the attitudes (or at least the behavior) of those who hired or sold to the poor" (Haveman 1977, p. 3).

In order to accomplish these goals a "massive tax cut" was proposed to "increase the nation's rate of growth and reduce unemployment." To increase the skills of the poor, Job Corps, Neighborhood Youth Corps, the Manpower Development and Training Act, Jobs, and WIN were established or expanded. Other efforts to improve the productivity of the poor related to raising their educational levels and health standards. To accomplish the first, Head Start, Upward Bound, Follow Through, Teachers Corps, and so on were established. For the second, Neighborhood Health Centers and Medicaid were approved. In order to change attitudes about hiring the poor, the Community Act program was designed to "restructure the social institutions by which the poor gained access to jobs and goods and services."

These programs reflected a definition of poverty which suggested that it could be alleviated if "the performance of the economy and the characteristics of the poor could be altered" (Haveman 1977, p. 6). If, however, the problem had been defined in terms of a "concern with the disparity in economic status between groups in society," public policy would have changed from "What will it do for the poor?" to "How will its benefits and costs be distributed among high and low income groups?" Concern with the "nature, causes and cures of poverty" would have been augmented "with the nature, causes, and cures of opulence" (Haveman 1977, p. 10).

Limited Resources and Competing Goals

The stress a value system places on how the nature of a problem is defined also guides decisions about which policies to adopt when there are limited resources and competing social problems. Yet, it is apparent that these factors exercise their own influence over the policies chosen for problem alleviation.

Every society is faced with limitations upon its resources which may divert public policies from their logical goals. The most dramatic illustration of this situation is the "guns vs. butter" alternative with which both war and peacetime economies are faced. During the Vietnam War, President Johnson attempted to continue both the War on Poverty and the War on Vietnam. (For a detailed analysis of the War on Poverty programs see Haveman 1977.) Most agree, however,

that the goal of alleviating poverty ultimately became secondary to Vietnam.*
Even in peacetime, societies must make judgments regarding what percentage of
existing resources should be devoted to defense as compared to social welfare
expenditures. Other pressures also exist given limited resources. A variety of
separate social problem areas relating to housing, health care, education, and so
on may receive unequal or minimal attention because of competition for existing
resources judged to be inadequate for comprehensive problem alleviation.

Whether a policy actually alleviates a specific defined social problem may be
affected by the existence of competing policy goals addressing interrelated problems. For example, the two social problems unemployment and inflation are
significantly interrelated, and what is done to relieve one may be contraindicated
for the other. Unemployment may be relieved by a deliberate governmental
policy of providing public employment and encouraging private industry to
provide jobs. However, such a policy may tend to fuel inflation by providing
more people with money. Under these circumstances, the most likely policy may
be one which attempts in limited fashion to resolve both problems somewhat
while not aggravating the other. As a result, the problem of unemployment will
be approached cautiously because of concern about inflation while the problem
of inflation will be approached with a concomitant concern about the problem
of unemployment. The result may be that neither problem is relieved satisfactorily.

The Policy Formulation Process

There are many views of what constitutes a social problem and, as a result,
a variety of pressures upon those who make decisions about which public policy
to follow. As a result, policy decisions tend to be made on the basis of "political
feasibility," or "disjointed incrementalism." Political feasibility suggests that
policies will be chosen on the basis of what is possible given the pressures to
which decision makers are subjected (Rein 1974, p. 66). It is an approach to
policy formulation which centers on "how to redistribute resources to politically weak and inarticulate groups in the interest of justice without producing
political and social instability, violence, and revolution" (Rein 1974, p. 66).
Disjointed incrementalism, a step-by-step movement of policy, is a closely
related technique of policy formulation which implicitly accepts the view that
"in the end muddling and compromise are the only rational approaches to the
management of conflicting and ambiguous goals" (Rein 1974, p. 66; and
Lindblom 1959).

---

*There is some disagreement on this point. However, Robert Lampman notes that the
negative view about the War on Poverty "arises from escalation of standards and the introduction of new ideas about what we ought to be doing." Haveman is in agreement with this
assessment (see Haveman 1977, pp. 1-19, 54).

The importance of political feasibility and disjointed incrementalism is that they are processes which tend to provide less than complete policy for amelioration of social problems. They reflect various approaches to social problem definition and the pressures that inhibit logical policy development, such as limited resources and competing pressures. Consequently, the existence of political feasibility and disjointed incrementalism provide the policy analyst with significant clues as to the direction which public policy assumes.

FACTORS INFLUENCING SOCIAL PROGRAMS

Just as social policy is supposed to mirror social problems, social programs are supposed to reflect social policy since they are the mechanism for carrying out policy. However, congruence between programs and policies may be affected by uncertainty about legislative intent, the existence of multifaceted approaches to single social problems, and the process of administrative implementation.

Legislative Intent

Legislative intent regarding the direction a program is to take is not stated obviously in typical statutory enactments. There may be a preamble or a statement of broad intentions regarding a program, but such information is usually insufficient for providing much insight into what legislators hoped to accomplish. For this reason it is usually necessary to look to the policy formulation process for clues. However, policy formulation can occur over a period of years and, as we know, reflects a multitude of pressures and views about what constitutes appropriate policy.

We suggested earlier that policy formulation may be an incremental process and that as a consequence approaches to problem solution may change over time. The difficulty, as we have noted, is that change is often "disjointed." As a result, original policy goals exist alongside newer approaches to problem solution. Social programs suffer in that they can be in congruence with an earlier policy for problem solution but out of step with a later one.

The Social Security Act of 1935 was originally designed to closely resemble a private insurance plan. As a result, the concept stressed that "each worker should receive at least as much in benefits as he had contributed" (Munnell 1977, p. 5). This emphasis upon "individual equity" is key to any private insurance plan since "workers would not choose to participate in a plan that failed to compensate them fairly for their contributions" (Munnel 1977, p. 6).

But the fact is that Social Security is *social* insurance, "where universal and compulsory protection is the goal" (Munnell 1977, p. 6). In partial recognition of this, the 1939 amendments to the act emphasized the concept of "social adequacy," that is, that benefits should be measured "not against lifetime contributions but rather a standard of living beneath which society feels no one should fall." As a result, minimum benefits are "very high relative to minimum contributions; dependent benefits have been added and have grown; and a progressive benefit structure is heavily weighted in favor of those low earnings workers who contribute the least to the system" (Munnell 1977, pp. 6-7).

This situation has led to confusion as to whether the Social Security Act should be assessed as a program designed to redistribute income to the poor or a program whose purpose is to be a "compulsory savings mechanism with certain insurance attributes" (Munnell 1977, p. 7). Under these circumstances, it is difficult to evaluate whether the program is providing appropriate aid to its targeted population given the uncertainty about the kind of policy to follow. It is difficult to tell whether the program matches the policy since it is unclear which policy it is supposed to reflect.

A major point in our analysis is that changes in emphasis over the years for the disability insurance program have resulted in confusion about the program's purpose. As we will discuss more fully later, when disability insurance was approved in 1956, legislative intent seems to have been aimed at restricting the potential universe of people who might be entitled to benefits. Thus, benefits were provided only for those between 50 and 65 years of age who were afflicted with a permanent disability which prevented substantial work. The disability had to result in death or be of "long, continued, and indefinite duration." Recipients had to wait six months before receiving benefits to rule out the possibility that their disability was only temporary. A heavy emphasis was put on rehabilitating disabled workers so that they could return to the labor force if at all possible.

However, this restrictive policy seems to have been altered in later years by one which suggests a more lenient attitude about who is entitled to benefits. As the 1939 amendments to the Social Security Act provided benefits to the dependents of retired workers, later amendments extended benefits to the dependents of the disabled. Additional amendments provided disability benefits for those under 50 years of age. Disabled widows and dependent widowers now also are eligible for reduced benefits at age 50 (Consulting Group on Welfare Reform 1977).

As if to reaffirm its original emphasis on a more restrictive policy regarding entitlement to benefits, Congress amended the program after a decade of operation to provide that benefits not be given unless it were proven that an applicant was unable to engage in any substantial gainful activity existing in the area in which the claimant lived or "in several regions of the country." It also provided that determination of ability to engage in substantial gainful activity should be "without regard as to whether a specific job vacancy exists for him, or whether he would be hired if he had applied for work" (Consulting Group on Welfare Reform 1977, pp. 6-7). This position was taken in order to counteract the impact of a court decision (*Kerner* v. *Flemming,* 283F. 2d916 [Sec.

Cir. 1960]), which held that "mere theoretical ability to engage in substantial gainful activity is not enough if no reasonable opportunity is available." Congress apparently was concerned that this would convert the disability insurance program into "a limited unemployment compensation program" (Consulting Group on Welfare Reform 1977, p. 7).

Given these changes over time the question is whether disability insurance is supposed to reflect the original, more restrictive policy or later modifications which seem to have opened the program to broader population groups and under conditions which may be less stringent than those originally intended. What should be made of the apparent aberration in the trend toward liberality, the provision which seems to reassert the original emphasis on ability to work?

Multi-faceted Approaches to Social Problems

What we have suggested is that policy guidance for particular programs can become convoluted over the years making congruence between the original underlying problem, policy, and program uncertain. An additional dilemma is that there are multifaceted approaches to single social problems.

As an example, the economic problems of the aged in the United States have been defined generally in terms of their need for income maintenance and assistance in meeting the costs of medical care. This definition has resulted in turn in at least two policy approaches to problem alleviation which exist side by side. Thus, income deficiencies are remedied by a policy of providing for universal contributory social insurance so that, upon retirement or death, benefits are provided based upon an earned right principle, that is, the worker's contributions for retirement or survivor benefits. Income deficiencies also are approached from the perspective that supplementation should be geared to need, that is to say, noncontributory and based on income or means testing. The need for medical care likewise is dealt with using these two policy approaches.

These multidimensional policies for meeting the income and medical care needs of the aged have resulted in overlapping programs. OASI and Medicare provide income maintenance through retirement and survivors benefits and health care financing based on the principles of social insurance. SSI, Medicaid, food stamps, and housing subsidies provide cash benefits, medical care financing, and in-kind aid based on income or means-tested financial need. The "overlapping" of these separate policies and programs on populations and problems is inevitable, but sometimes it results in conflict and confusion rather than coordinated assistance for populations in meeting multi-problem situations.

Administrative Decision Making

The administrative decision-making process used for program implementation is important because administration is not merely a mechanical process but one in which stated policy objectives can be redefined by a process of administrative implementation which sets the limits and defines the reality of what is programmatically feasible. The amount of administrative redefinition of policy objectives for programs is dependent upon the extent to which policy is specified in the law, the magnitude of administrative rule-making discretion, and the prevalence of group pressures upon an agency. We have already suggested that typical legislative enactments contain only nominal instruction about the policy intent of an act. Given this situation and the disinclination of legislatures to assume responsibility for the details of policy implementation, the potential for administrative discretion is great. This is especially so given the multifaceted direction which public policy can take.

A major result of this situation is that administrative agencies are free to issue rules and regulations for program implementation which reflect their approximation of legislative policy intent. As we will discuss in greater detail later, the expressed intent of the legislation authorizing the SSDI program emphasized that an inability to work (engage in substantial gainful activity) because of medically determinable impairment entitled an eligible applicant to benefits. Over the years, and without specific congressional approval, rules have been implemented which seem to have changed the basis for receiving benefits. The obvious point of concern is whether this change represents independent administrative policy making or a correct interpretation of congressional intent.

Even assuming that guidelines coincide with legislative policy intent, agency personnel enjoy considerable freedom of interpretation. This is why such stress is placed upon employing highly professional people who presumably understand the necessity of abiding by such guidelines.* One of our concerns is to determine whether administrative interpretation of the disability determination guidelines has resulted in the replacement of the policy that benefits should be denied if the applicant can work with one that suggests that benefits should be provided if substantial need exists and that the nature of a disability should be considered in that context.

Our discussion of problem definition and policy formulation has suggested the importance of different perspectives in influencing the direction each takes. These perspectives are also an important influence upon the administrative decision-making process. If they reflect the major groups constituting the population affected by the problem, as defined in the policy framing, the program administrative decisions will likely coincide with legislative intent. If, however, some groups have greater access and control over an administrative agency than others, then decisions about who gets benefits may differ from the original policy intent and result in a deprivation of benefits for those defined as

---

*We will look at the importance of professionalism as a deterrent to excessive administrative discretion in Chapter 5.

constituting the needy population.* This is what Herbert Simon means when he refers to the "environmental situation" which "inevitably limits the alternatives that are available."

RELATIONSHIP BETWEEN PROBLEM, POLICY, AND PROGRAM IN DISABILITY

The underlying objective of public social welfare programs should be to provide relief for those directly affected by a problem.

Ideally, the most successful problem relief is provided when there is symmetry among the social problems affecting population groups, the policies designed to meet those social problems, and the specifications of the programs and their implementing procedures offered to provide amelioration. The point of concern in our present analysis is to determine which factors contribute to and which diminish this idealized relationship.

Fundamentally, the degree of congruence among problem, policy, and program depends upon how adequately a social problem is defined. If there is an accurate appraisal of the nature of a social problem, it is more likely that a public policy and the program to implement it will reflect this accuracy and that some measure of problem relief will be forthcoming. A limited definition of the problem may result in perfect congruence between the policy and the program designed to achieve it but still not deal effectively with the social problem. In the case of the Social Security Disability Insurance program, the problem of disability was defined from the perspective of the individual and family financial difficulties resultant from a previously employed worker's inability to engage in substantial gainful activity caused by a physical or mental impairment. The policy formulated to deal with this situation called for the provision of cash benefits to disabled workers covered under the Social Security system. While rehabilitation was emphasized, the primary focus was on the benefits to be paid. The problem and policy conception did not address the need to provide employment opportunities as the major issue but rather saw the inability to work among the disabled as distinct from other forms of unemployment or underemployment. The program established a disability insurance cash benefit with disability determinations made at the state level using presumably uniform national standards. These standards focused on the medical documentation of listed impairments or their equivalents as the primary basis for identifying the existence of a disability.

In the remainder of this chapter, we will review the techniques used to obtain data on which to base our analysis. The balance of this book discusses

---

*Several authors have written on the relative importance and effect of pressure groups. For Example, see Bentley (1949), Truman (1951), and Dahl (1961).

the Social Security Disability Insurance program from the analytic perspective of the consistency in problem, policy, and program focus. This approach suggests that the goal of social programs — to provide significant relief for populations affected by problems — can be stymied by inappropriate problem definition, inadequate policy formulation, and inconsistent program specification and implementation.

METHODOLOGY OF DATA DEVELOPMENT

A variety of different approaches were utilized in assembling the material presented here. They are discussed briefly in this section under the following categories: Identification of Problem, Policy Formulation and Program Development, and Model Analysis.

Identification of Problem

There are two general ways to assess the prevalence of disability. First is through the rates of application for and allowance of disability benefits in the various programs of disability insurance, compensation, and assistance. This approach is beset with a number of shortcomings. All disabled people do not apply to such programs, nor do the gatekeeping decisions in these programs represent valid criteria for the identification and evaluation of disability. Many people whose health conditions meet the disability criteria of programs for which they are covered continue to work in spite of their impairments, at times at the risk of endangering their health. On the other hand, there are those who are allowed benefits on the basis of current criteria in many programs but who are actually capable of competitive employment (Nagi 1969-b). Furthermore, program statistics are likely to include multiple counts of individuals who are eligible for benefits under more than one program.

The second approach is through representative surveys which seek information from probability samples about their disabilities. Among the most significant of these surveys are those conducted periodically by the Social Security Administration, the United States Census of 1970 and 1980, and the Health Interview Survey (HIS) conducted by the National Center for Health Statistics (NCHS). Other national surveys were conducted by government agencies and independent researchers. These surveys vary in the age definitions of their populations and in sampling designs. Some employ screening instruments, reserving detailed interviews for those identified as disabled and limited in ability, while others conduct detailed interviews with the total sample. The surveys vary in the specifics of concepts, questions, indicators, and indexes they use and produce.

One common feature is that they all depend on laymen's reports for themselves or for others in their households. Laymen's reports represent only one set of definitions of disability which vary from those of professionals in various concerned disciplines. A comparison between physicians' assessments of disability and those given independently by laymen for themselves show a fairly high degree of consistency (Nagi 1969-a). As will be seen later, the different surveys of disability in the United States produce fairly similar prevalence estimates.

The prevalence and incidence of impairment and pathology are more difficult to estimate on the basis of laymen's reports. Through the HIS, the NCHS attempts to collect information on the prevalence of various impairments and pathology. They also collect such data on the basis of Health Examination Surveys (HES), in which a subsample is actually given a medical assessment. Comparisons between the results of the HIS and the HES show the inadequacy of the laymen's reports (U.S., Department of Health, Education, and Welfare, NCHS 1961). It should be noted that data on incidence are much less available because they are difficult to obtain. Since incidence rates represent new cases contracting a given disease or disorder over a period of time, very specific design and recordkeeping is necessary for their estimation. The best available sources for such data are registries established for certain diseases, but their utility for disability programs is doubtful. The most appropriate sources of data for actuarial and other program purposes would be the records of temporary disability insurance concerning short-term pathology and national disability surveys concerning conditions of long or continued duration.

Data on the income of the disabled can be obtained from the national disability surveys mentioned above. The census, the SSA, and other surveys seek detailed information on levels and sources of earnings, income from public programs, and income from all other sources. They commonly differentiate the earnings and other incomes of the respondents from those of the family or household. Impacts of disability on family income must take into account the loss of earnings of the respondent, the loss of earnings of other members of the household who withdraw from or limit their participation in the labor market in order to provide care for the disabled, and the additional earnings of members of the household who may enter the labor market in order to supplement the family income. Data on income are among the least reliable when reported by laymen for themselves. It is difficult to verify the reported income even for the SSA surveys since the SSA's records include data on earnings only up to the level of the maximum taxable under the program.

From the perspective of our present concern, the most significant impacts of disability are on employment and earnings. Data about the influence on earnings can be found in the national surveys. They should be interpreted with caution because of the limitations pointed out above. The total economic impacts of disability can be evaluated through two components. One is the loss in earnings sustained by the disabled; data on this aspect are lacking. The other dimension is the aggregate of transfer payments made through programs of disability insurance, compensation, and assistance. The cost of services to the disabled should be a component of this last measure. Data on this aspect are easier to obtain from public programs, which issue periodical reports about transfer payments and costs of services, than from the private insurance sector.

Finally, information on employment constitutes a common feature of disability surveys. Some limit their questions to the employment status at the time of data collection while others seek more complete information about work status and work history, concentrating on the influence of disability and other health conditions on the work patterns of respondents.*

Policy Formulation and Program Development

Assessing the intent of policy makers or tracing the development of a specific program involves interpretation and extrapolation as well as a consideration of the writings of others. What is intended for a policy is not always specified. Sometimes it has to be read into the statements and actions of individuals. Often an after-the-fact determination of policy intent is essentially a consensus of opinion among various commentators. This is particularly the case if there is clear, explicit statement of policy. In any event, the processes of assessing policy intent and tracing program development emerge as searches for and study of documents and statements rather than a systematic analysis of data.

In considering policy formulation and program development for the Social Security Disability Insurance program we have reviewed the writings of knowledgeable individuals who were active in the original efforts to plan the provision of social insurance in this country. The earlier debates on the merits and problems involved in including disability coverage under social security also have been reviewed because of their implications for the form the program ultimately took. The recommendations of various advisory groups and committees are discussed for the same reason. These various documents provide an account of the positions taken by different individuals and groups and help explain some of the compromises incorporated into the policy and program. Commentaries on the policy issues and debates are also a valuable source of information on how others have viewed these items. The same is true of the commentaries and analyses on the form and function of the program itself.

The development of the program, from its initial passage in 1954 as a freeze on entitlement to retirement benefits so that such entitlement would not be lost because of disability through the first limited program of disability benefits per se in 1956, to the current, more liberalized program, is traced in the various

---

*See, for example, the difference between the surveys conducted by the SSA, which devotes considerable space to work status and history, and those of the NCHS, which are fairly limited in this respect.

hearings, reports, and ultimately passed and implemented amendments. These documents provide a chronological history of the program and the changes that have occurred since its inception.

Specific policy pronouncements are found less commonly after a program's initial consideration and passage. However, the changes made in later program modifications, even those presumably made for administrative or equity reasons, have substantial, if not as easily recognized, implications for the original policy which guided program development. Careful review of these changes permits us to assess the degree of consistency in program development beyond the initial plan with reference to the policy it was designed to implement.

An additional item with substantial implications for the conduct of a program and for the degree to which it meets the intended policy is the set of regulations issued by the agency with operating responsibility. These regulations are supposed to establish the guidelines for program administration. However, implementing regulations can alter the intent of policy and program under the guise of operating efficiency, regularity, and simplicity. These regulations and changes in them will be reviewed also for their impact on the original policy and program intent.

Model Analysis

Assessing the interaction among problem, policy, and program in reviewing the attempt to meet the needs of the disabled through social insurance requires our analysis of data not collected for this specific purpose. The policy analysis framework we are using was applied after the fact to the primary body of data to be presented here. However, the fact that the research was not initiated for the specific purpose of the public policy analysis for which it is used here does not diminish its relevance for policy and program planning. It is necessary, under these circumstances, for us to draw policy implications out of the data and analysis beyond what was recognized in the material's original use.

Our approach here is to assess the congruity between an underlying problem and the policy formulated to deal with it and between a policy and the program developed to implement it. We have already expressed the relationships this type of analysis entails for the area of disability and discussed the types of data to be used for identifying the nature and scope of the problem and for chronicling the setting of policy and the enactment and implementation of legislation establishing a program of insurance benefits for the disabled under Social Security. In the analysis of the congruity among problem, policy, and program, we will be using data from a study of the ecology of disability, that is, an assessment of the relationship between the characteristics of the area in which people live and the rate of disability in the area. Two points of concern provided the original incentive for this ecological study: the growth of the Social Security Disability Insurance program in both numbers of persons on the disability insurance rolls and the amount of benefit dollars paid,* and recognition of the importance of social and environmental conditions in ameliorating the effect of physical handicaps (Haber 1967).

The underlying conceptual rationale for the analysis is that disability is socially and economically defined and is based on an existent impairment which potentially limits functional capacity. The impairment leads to a disability when it results in the individual either not being able to perform or not being accepted to perform specific expected job functions. Since the majority of working-age Americans have one or more chronic diseases,† there is a vast reservoir of persons who could be defined as disabled if the demands of their environments exceeded, or were thought to exceed, their capacities.

The primary concern in looking at socioeconomic characteristics is as they might affect the general conditions of life or the actual or perceived opportunities for employment for persons with work-related limitations, that is, area factors that might influence the aggregate rate of impaired persons who have or perceive themselves to have difficulty getting and holding a job and who, therefore, might consider themselves disabled and apply for and be awarded SSDI benefits.

Our interest is in the disabled self-concept as influenced by the socioeconomic environment. No attempt is made in this analysis to deal with the issue of whether socioeconomic factors relate to rates of disability on an objective basis, rational economic and social assessments, or a subjective basis, the social-psychological-environmental impact. The primary focus of analysis is the disability policy and program approach which implies that a definition as disabled is based on individual capacity, that is, medically definable impairment plus personal vocational factors, but not by the objective or subjective impact of the socioeconomic environment.

Sources and Use of Data

A limited opportunity to study the association between a range of social and economic characteristics and area disability rates was provided by the fact that the U.S. Census of Population, in 1970, included for the first time a series of questions on work disability for persons aged 14 to 64 as part of the five-percent sample questionnaire. A limitation in the data's usefulness is the fact that they do not provide the opportunity for an analysis over time. The data are for 1970 only. However, within this limitation the data provide the most comprehensive array of cross-sectional data on area characteristics and rates of disability available anywhere.

*Periodic *Monthly Benefits Statistics* reports issued by the Office of Research and Statistics, Social Security Administration, Department of Health, Education, and Welfare.
†See various NCHS publications on chronic conditions from the National Health Survey.

The 1970 census was not the first time national data had been collected on work-limiting disability. As mentioned earlier, the Social Security Administration has conducted a program of national surveys of disabled adults since 1966, and the National Health Survey conducted by the National Center for Health Statistics has collected data on disability for many years.

The Social Security Administration surveys facilitate estimates of the incidence and prevalence of work-limiting disability using a definition including several levels of severity. These data have been analyzed to determine various social and economic characteristics of the disabled, with a concern for items that might either dispose towards or result from disability.

However, these survey data provide for only a very limited analysis of differences among geographic areas in rates of disability, including application for and receipt of social security disability benefits, or of the relationships between characteristics of these areas and rates of disability. Such an analysis, even using data collected after almost 15 years of program operation, can shed light on whether the assumptions built into the policy for dealing with disability are meaningful in terms of their implications about the nature of work disability and the working population's use of this phenomenon.

The 1970 census data give us an opportunity to consider the relationship between disability and a variety of other factors which is not possible using samples that were not selected to provide representation from states and smaller areas. For the first time, we have national data on rates of disability by state, county, and city. Aggregate data on disability by severity can be related to various area social and economic characteristics to determine whether any association exists between such factors and these rates of disability.*

The 1970 Census of Population questionnaire asked for each person aged 14-64 in the five-percent sample whether

> they had a health condition or disability which limited the kind or amount of work they could do at a job and whether their health prevented them from doing any work at all. Persons who answered "yes" to either or both questions were classified as *disabled*; persons who responded that they had a disability but were not prevented from doing any work at all as *disabled, able to work*; persons who responded their health prevented them from doing any work at all as *disabled, cannot work* . . . persons who indicated they had a disability affecting the kind or amount of work they could do on the job were asked how long they had been disabled." (U.S. Department of Commerce 1972)

Data on area social and economic characteristics used in this analysis are also from the 1970 census.

---

*The data permit a limited disaggregation of the disability rate by demographic characteristics. Separate rates were computed and analyzed by age group, race, sex, and education.

Data on the rate of application for Social Security Disability Insurance benefits were analyzed for their relationship to various area social and economic characteristics. Data on the rate of award of these benefits were analyzed for their relationship to a series of administrative characteristics of the SSDI disability determination process for these benefits as it is differentially operated within each state. Social Security Administration program data were used to measure State Disability Determining Unit administrative characteristics and rates of applications and awards for this analysis. The major source for these data was the July 1974 *Committee Staff Report on the Disability Insurance Program* issued by the Committee on Ways and Means of the U.S. House of Representatives.

While we have used the term "applications," technically the program measure used in analysis is "initial determinations." The distinction is that applications from persons who are not covered for disability insurance benefits are not reviewed for substantive merit, in other words, there is no disability determination. For our purposes, such applications are not analytically or programmatically significant. Therefore, as we use the term, "applications" refers only to those claims of disability considered on the basis of their merits and excludes those disallowed because the person lacks program coverage.

Similarly, the term "award" of SSDI benefits is used as a convenience for the program measure used which is approval of the application based on a substantive determination of disability that prohibits substantial gainful activity. Technically, an approval does not become an award until the actual payment authorizing has been completed and benefits start. However, for our purposes, what is meaningful is an approval of the application based on its merits as a claim for disability.

Since the disability determination process is operated separately within each state by a state agency, it is conceptually more meaningful to analyze the programmatic data at this level. While the state is not the only geographic level available for the analysis of the relationship between area characteristics and rates of self-defined disability, it does represent a socially, politically, and economically definable unit which is highly relevant for this purpose. Since the two parts of the study are interrelated and the state data are uniquely appropriate for the programmatic analysis, it was decided to use the state as the primary level of geographic concern for both aspects of the analysis.*

Approximately 50 variables measuring the socioeconomic and demographic characteristics of states were considered in preliminary analysis. Included were variables descriptive of the state's specific industrial and occupational specializations. The final selection of variables included to represent the socioeconomic

---

*See Appendix A for a list of all the variables used in our analysis with their identifying variable numbers separated into SSA Program Measures and Administrative Variables, and Census Disability Measures and Socioeconomic Characteristics. Appendix B lists the input data used in the major analyses by variable number by state.

characteristic of a state was based on an examination of these preliminary analyses on both theoretical and empirical grounds. As a result, certain variables anticipated to be of critical importance in explaining state-to-state variance in disability rates, such as measures of specific industrial specialization, were dropped from the analysis because they lacked predictive power, and global indexes were left in to measure these areas more generally. On the other hand, specific variables of conceptual interest, for example, state unemployment rate, for which no reasonable alternatives were apparent, were left in although they did not appear significant for the explanation of variance in disability rates.

Ten variables were finally selected for use in the analysis because of their presumed measurement of a state's general socioeconomic circumstances and their potential impact upon the actual or perceived receptivity to labor force participation by the disabled. Those ten variables are: percent of males under 65 in labor force; percent of females under 65 in labor force; percent of labor force self-employed or unpaid family worker; percent working under 15 hours a week; percent of labor force unemployed; percent of labor force with less than a ninth-grade education; index of industrial diversity of labor force; index of occupational diversity of labor force; percent of families earning under $4,000, earner present; and percent of families with Social Security income.

For all ten variables the disabled population was removed prior to the computation of the variable as a rate. This resulted in a set of variables uncontaminated by the relative size of the disabled population within the state. While a valid argument can be made for the disabled being a part of the population in a disabled person's state of residence, their removal from these independent variables eliminates the suspicion that any relationships found between them and the rates of disability are the result of the confounding effect of the disabled population being measured in both the independent and dependent variables.

The last two variables in the list are more general measures of the state's economic and social condition. The last variable, "percent of families with Social Security income," becomes a proxy for the size of the over-65 population, since the disabled are excluded.

This socioeconomic "model" results in the following predictions for the direction of relationship of the independent variables with the disability rates of concern: high rates of families with less than $4,000 income, families with Social Security income, and unemployment, and high percentages of persons in the labor force with less than a ninth-grade education reflect less favorable conditions and should be associated with higher rates of disability; and high rates of male and female labor force participation and part-time and self-employment and high levels of industrial and occupational diversity are all indicative of more favorable socioeconomic conditions and a labor force structure which may be more "congenial" for participation by persons with work-related limitations and should, therefore, be associated with lower rates of disability.

These ten variables were used in an analysis of the relationship between state socioeconomic characteristics and the measures of disability. Multiple regressions were run using the Statistical Package for the Social Sciences (SPSS). The nature of the research problem fits this statistical analysis model. The technique is a powerful tool which can discern how well a set of independent variables predict variation in a dependent variable and how important each variable is in the resulting prediction equation. Studying each effect separately would be a distortion of the nature of the disability process. The multiple regression technique, insofar as the effects are additive, is designed to capture this process.*

---

*For substantiation of this view, see Kerlinger and Pedhazur (1973, p. 4), in which they hold that there is a complex interaction of independent variables impinging upon a dependent variable.

2
STATEMENT OF THE PROBLEM

CONCEPTUAL ISSUES

Before attempting to explore the dimensions, and assess the magnitude of the problem of disability, it will be useful to clarify the concept of disability and distinguish it from related but separable concepts: pathology, impairment, and limitation in capacity. We find a fourfold conceptual scheme presented by Nagi in 1963, and tested in subsequent research, to provide an appropriate framework for this analysis (Nagi 1965).

The state of active pathology may result from infections, metabolic imbalances, degenerative disease processes, trauma, or other causes. It is associated with the mobilization of defenses and coping mechanisms. Such a condition involves two conceptually distinct phenomena: the interruption of normal processes and the simultaneous efforts of the organism to restore a normal state of existence. More than the surrender to an abnormal state of affairs, pathology is also the fight for health (Selye 1956). In modern health practice, the surgical elimination of defective parts, the administration of medications, and other types of therapy aid the organism in its fight. Such interventions may become necessary over a long period or even, as in some chronic diseases, indefinitely.

The concept of impairment indicates a physiological, anatomical, or mental loss or other abnormality, or both. When impairments do not involve active pathology, for example, when they are abnormalities and residual losses remaining after the active stage of a disease, nonpathological congenital deformities, and conditions resulting from the disuse of muscles for extended periods, the distinctions between impairment and pathology become more meaningful. Although every pathology involves an impairment, not every impairment involves a pathology.

The most direct way impairments contribute to disability is through the limitations in function or capacity they effect. These limitations vary in the level of organization at which they are manifested. Many tissues can exist with altered structures or functions without imposing any limitations on the functioning of the organism as a whole. For example, a significant number of muscle fibers must become denervated for discernible weakness to occur. Much alteration in the wall of blood vessels can take place before appreciable changes ensue in the flow within these vessels. An infinite number of similar examples could be cited. In general, one could speak of functional limitations at the levels of molecules, cells, tissues, organs, regions, systems, or the whole organism. Although limitations at a lower level of organization may not be reflected in higher levels, the reverse is not true. An individual who is unable to reach overhead because of tightness in the shoulder can be expected also to have abnormalities at the levels of tissues and cells that make up the shoulder. It is important to note that functional limitations at higher levels of organization may result from differing impairments and functional limitations at the lower levels. For example, the inability to lift a heavy weight may be related to mechanical problems in the lumbosacral region, or it may be the result of diminished cardiac output or pulmonary ventilation (Melvin and Nagi 1970). Limitations of function can be grouped into four categories: physical, including such activities as walking, climbing, reaching, lifting, bending, stooping, and the use of hands and fingers; mental, referring to intellectual and reasoning abilities; emotional, meaning the ability to cope with life stresses and adjustments; and sensory, such as vision and hearing.

Disability is a form of inability or limitation in performing roles and tasks expected of an individual within a social environment. These tasks and roles are organized by spheres of life activities, such as self-care, education, family relations, recreation, economic life, and employment. Although short-term sickness may be disabling for a brief period, the term disability is usually applied to inabilities of long or continued duration. It may be associated with the presence of active pathology or with remaining impairments after pathology has been controlled or eliminated, as in the case of healed amputations or residual paralyses. It should be apparent that not every impairment results in disability, and similar patterns of disability may result from different types of impairment and limitation in function. Furthermore, identical types of impairment and limitations in function with similar degrees of severity may result in different patterns of disability, depending upon both the reactions of the disabled and the social definition of the situation. This indicates that the development of disability, like that of most complex phenomena, can be explained only through multiple causal models and therefore can be identified and measured only by multiple indicators.

From the viewpoint of formulating public policy, disabilities in work and independent living are particularly significant. The first often leads to economic dependency and the second to other forms of dependency. Concern in this presentation is primarily with work disability, which can be defined from varying perspectives. Particularly important are self-definitions, which constitute the basis for people's behavior and represent the data reported in the census and other surveys, and the definitions of those organizations administering benefits and services. Differences between these two perspectives on what constitutes work disability is the primary reason behind the elaborate and costly systems and procedures for determining eligibility and entitlement to benefits and services.

A concern for work disability results in focusing on persons of working age who might otherwise be gainfully employed. This excludes children and the aged who usually are not defined as working-age populations. It also results in excluding definitions of the problem of disability that do not relate to employment. While other government policies and programs do deal with disability in children and the aged and view disability from other perspectives, this is not the case for the policy underlying the Social Security Disability Insurance program or for the specifics of the program itself. A program of childhood disability benefits under Social Security does pay benefits for persons age 18 or over who have been work-disabled since childhood. However, this is a recognition of the continued dependency status of such persons. Benefits are paid only on the account of a parent who is deceased or entitled to disability or retirement benefits and based on dependency upon that parent. Benefits are not paid under the program because of the childhood disability itself but only because of this continued dependency.

Limitations in the capacity to perform work-related functions among children is a concern for education, training, and rehabilitation programs. These efforts are heavily oriented toward ultimate work capacity or, at a minimum, self-care. General capacities, such as self-care and mobility, are of concern relative to persons of all ages, including children, the aged, and those of working age. Limitations in these areas are an alternate perspective for the definition of disability and are of policy and program concern independent of work capacity. However, they are not relevant to the policy and program under discussion.

The definitions provided above regarding impairments, limitations in function, and disability are of critical concern in this policy and program distinction. Limitations in expected normal adult functioning because of physical or mental impairments which do not compromise work capacity are not work-disabling. Only if work capacity is interfered with does the situation meet the definition of disability of concern here.

Even within a concern for work capacity separable policy and program approaches are possible. The problem could be addressed from the perspective of restoration of individual work capacity, restructuring the work environment or performance demands to compensate for capacity limitations, or earnings replacement through programs of private or public income maintenance. The Social Security program for disabled workers focuses on the economic impact of work disability and provides cash benefits to replace a portion of lost earnings. The program officially encourages rehabilitation and return to gainful employment and provides a percentage of the benefit amount paid in each state to a fund for the vocational rehabilitation of beneficiaries. However, the program itself directly pays benefits only.

Other programs also provide financial benefits for disability but with more limited population or situational restrictions on their definitions of disability. Briefly, veteran's benefits are paid for service-connected illness or injury based on the extent of damage to the individual. If, in addition, the individual is unable to work, a higher benefit amount is paid. Workers' compensation pays for illness or injury sustained because of the job. The Supplemental Security Income program uses the same definition of work disability as does SSDI but applies a test of economic need.

The SSDI program of cash benefits is for all covered workers who meet the disability standards without regard to the circumstances under which they became disabled or their financial circumstances as long as they are not engaged in substantial gainful activity. A primary concern in regard to assessment of the program, and one we will return to later, is the heavy reliance on impairment standards as the equivalent of disability. This approach tends to obscure the impact of differences in individual characteristics and performance demands in determining whether an impairment in fact leads to a work disability.

PREVALENCE AND INCIDENCE

Several indicators and measures can be used to convey a picture of the magnitude of disability. Of these, three have been selected as comprising the most meaningful combination: the distributions of disabilities and related health problems and limitations of activity in the population; the economic impacts of disability upon individuals, families, and society; and the impacts of disability upon employment and labor supply.

The distribution of any characteristic in a population can be expressed in two different ways: prevalence and incidence. The rates of prevalence represent the number of cases having the characteristic in question in relation to the population at risk at a given time. Cross-sectional surveys provide the needed information for computing such rates. On the other hand, incidence rates refer to the number of new cases acquiring the characteristic in question (disability, disease, and so on) over a specified period of time in relation to the population at risk. Thus, meaningful data on incidence rates require repeated surveys and more complex specifications concerning the natural cycle of the characteristic under investigation. Attempts toward estimating the incidence rates of disability have been very limited and less than successful. Therefore, the distributions to be presented here are of prevalence rates.

It would seem to have been a reasonable expectation that there were current background data on the extent of disability in the United States at the time appropriate policy and program directions to deal with the issue were being considered. While some data did in fact exist on long-term work disability, there are two points to be recognized relative to these data. First, they were not collected specifically to provide data for the discussion on how to approach work disability. As a result, they were not collected just prior to any of the critical deliberations and did not gear themselves to definitions being considered as possible policy or program standards. Second, there seems to have been no use made of the data in the hearings on disability legislation or in efforts to set standards. It is particularly significant that, although the existence of a health impairment was used as the primary basis for determining the presence of a disability, no study has yet been made of the distribution of the impairments established as a disability standard nor the effect of these impairments on work capacity.

The National Health Survey conducted in the winter of 1935-36 was an earlier comprehensive effort to provide information on illness and disability. It was a one-visit, house-to-house survey and covered an urban sample of 2.5 million individuals. In an attempt at periodic assessment, the Social Security Board arranged for the inclusion of special questions to determine the number of persons disabled one day or more during the census week in connection with the Monthly Report on the Labor Force Surveys conducted in May, June, and August, 1942, and February 1943. These were more limited in scope than the 1935-36 survey (Moore and Sanders 1950).

In 1949, the Social Security Administration, the Office of Vocational Rehabilitation, and the Public Health Service combined forces to use the Bureau of the Census's Current Population Survey to obtain information on the numbers of disabled persons in the United States. Questions on disability were added to the survey in February 1949, and again in September 1950. These supplemental questions were asked only for persons aged 14-64. Disability was defined as follows:

> As used in this study, disabled persons are those who, on the day of enumeration, were unable to do their regular work or perform other duties because of disease or injury, as well as those who had a long-term

physical or mental condition that allowed them to work only occasion-
ally or not at all. Included within this definition are those persons who,
except for their disability, would have been engaged in gainful work
as members of the labor force, although the degree of their disability
might not have been such as to prevent them from going regularly to
school or doing housework in their own homes. Not included under this
concept would be, for example, a man who, although he had lost two
limbs as the result of an accident, was working on the day of the
enumeration and had been working regularly for some time. This
concept of disability was adopted because it appeared to be the most
practicable and would encompass those persons with whom the spon-
sors of the study and many other groups are particularly concerned.
(Moore and Sanders 1950, p. 8).

The data from the February 1949 and September 1950 surveys indicate
a decrease from 4.6 million to 3.6 million disabled persons (Sanders and Moore
1955). This was attributed to seasonal variability. However, for longer-term
disability, that is, disability lasting seven months or more, there was an almost
identical estimated number and rate. In February 1949, slightly over 2 million
persons were disabled for seven months or more. This was just over 2 percent of
the civilian non-institutionalized population aged 14-64. Approximately 80 percent of these disabled persons were not in the labor force (Moore and Sanders
1950). The differences in the overall rates for the two surveys were almost
entirely based on short-term disability for which "seasonal variation" is a more
logical explanation. About one-half the difference was based on the higher rate
of disability of one week or less in the February 1949 winter month (Sanders
and Moore 1955).

As we shall see shortly, these numbers and rates for "long-term" disability
are significantly lower than those resulting from more recent surveys. This is the
case despite the fact that all the definitional differences between the 1949-50
surveys and the later studies would suggest relatively higher rates should have
been found in these earlier studies. For example, the 1949-50 surveys used
inability to do regular work as the standard for disability, while later surveys
primarily used inability to do any work as the standard. The policy and program
considerations focused on inability to work, not inability to do regular work. No
pre-program studies concentrated on this issue.

Of the surveys and data files available for more recent information on
disability and related conditions, four are of particular significance in regard to
the non-institutionalized population of the United States: the Social Security
Administration's Surveys of Disabled Adults, the 1970 U.S. Census, the Health
Interview Surveys (HIS) conducted by the National Center for Health Statistics
(NCHS), and the 1972 Ohio State University's Survey.

The Social Security Administration's surveys of disabled adults make
important contributions to estimates of work disability. The first, conducted in

1966, included a probability sample of the U.S. civilian non-institutionalized population 18 through 64 years of age. The multiframe sample also included disability insurance beneficiaries under Social Security, recipients of public assistance because of blindness or "permanent and total disability," and applicants for disability insurance under Social Security. In these surveys, disability is defined as "limitation in the kind or amount of work (or housework) resulting from a chronic health condition or impairment lasting three or more months" (Haber 1967). A threefold classification was used in reporting the severity of work disability:

Severe Disability: Unable to work altogether or unable to work regularly.
Occupational Disability: Able to work regularly, but unable to do the same work as before the onset of disability or unable to work full time.
Secondary Work Limitations: Able to work full time, regularly, and keep the same occupation, but with limitations in the kind or amount of work they can perform; women with limitations in housekeeping but not in work are included as having secondary work limitations.

The SSA conducted another disability survey in 1972. While different in design, constituting a follow-up to the 1970 census responses to disablity questions, the 1972 survey was essentially similar to that of 1966 in its conceptual framework and operational definitions. The rates of disability reported in the two surveys are presented in Table 2.1. It should be noted that the 1972

TABLE 2.1
Rates of Work Disability Reported in the Social Security Administration's
Surveys of Disabled Adults

(percentage of population)

Severity of Disability	1966 Survey	1972 Survey
Severe	5.9	7.3
Occupational	4.9	3.3
Secondary Work Limitations	6.4	4.1
Total	17.2	14.7

survey includes persons ages 20 through 64. The findings of the 1970 census place the prevalence rates of work disability at 11.2 percent of the U.S. non-institutionalized population ages 16 through 64, with the "disabled, able to work" constituting 5.3 percent and the "disabled, cannot work" 5.9 percent (U.S., Department of Commerce, Bureau of the Census 1973, pp. 712-17). Considering that there were 104,556,480 in these age categories at the time of that census, these proportions mean that of a total of 11,710,326 disabled people, 5,541,493 were disabled, able to work and 6,168,832 disabled, cannot work.

Data on work disability are reported by the NCHS as part of "limitations in major activities." The 1974 findings of the HIS show that 10.2 percent of people 17 through 64 years of age had such limitations, including 2.6 percent who were "unable to carry on major activities" and 7.6 percent who were "limited in amount or kind of major activity" (U.S., Department of Health, Education, and Welfare, NCHS 1967). These distributions vary considerably from the two categories reported in the 1970 census and presented above. Closer to the census, however, are the HIS rates for males in the same ages which show 4.2 percent "unable to carry on major activity," and 6.2 percent "with limitation in amount or kind of major activity," for a total of 10.4 percent with limitations in major activities. It should be noted that the NCHS reports another category of limitations, "with limitation but not in major activity." These are defined to include participation in athletics and extracurricular activities on the part of school-age children, in church, clubs, and similar activities on the part of housewives, and in church, sports, clubs, and the like on the part of workers and all other persons.

The final set of figures to be presented here came from a national survey conducted by the Ohio State University in which the epidemiology of disability constituted a major component (Nagi 1976). Data for this survey were collected in 1972 from a probability sample of the non-institutionalized population of the continental United States (excluding Alaska). Questions concerning work disability were asked of persons between 18 and 64 years of age who comprised 5,332 respondents. A work disability index was constructed on the basis of these questions grouping respondents into three categories:

No Work Disability: Persons who are working regularly in jobs (36 hours or more), housekeeping, or school work, and reported no limitations in current or previous work.

Limited in Work Roles and Activities: Persons who are working regularly in jobs, housekeeping, or in school, but reported difficulties in performing their current work, a change in jobs, or part-time work because of disability.

Vocationally Disabled: Persons who are out of the labor market because of being disabled; are below 65 and have retired or left their last employment because of disability; or who cannot perform housekeeping or school work. This category includes a small number of persons who, because of health problems, were working on a limited part-time basis.

The rates of vocational disability in the population were found to be 6.3 percent and those of limitations in work roles and activities 4.4 percent, adding up to 10.7 percent. Work disability in this survey was identified and its severity measured in terms of actual work status and work history rather than on the basis of questions as to whether they can or cannot work.

Ignoring the slight age differences among these four sources of data, the most comparable categories and at the same time most important for this presentation are the rates of the severest categories of work disability. These include people who were "unable to carry on major activity" in the HIS; "disabled, cannot work" in the 1970 census; "severely disabled" in the SSA's 1966 and 1972 surveys of disabled adults; and "the vocationally disabled" in the Ohio State University's survey. The percentage rates classified in these categories were 2.6, 5.9, 5.9, 7.3, and 6.3, respectively. The NCHS estimates are much lower than the rest, most likely because of the ways questions are phrased and the survey context within which data on disability are collected. The 1972 SSA survey reports appreciably higher rates that cannot be explained merely by the older age composition (20 through 64 years, compared to the other surveys in which the lower age limit was 18 or younger). Considering the 7.3 percent rate of disability and the nearly 130 million people 17 through 64 years of age in the United States in 1977, the number of non-institutionalized vocationally disabled in that year would have been almost 9.5 million people.*

Although various forms of work are used as occupational therapy for inmates in many institutions, mental or physical limitations that require insti- tutionalization must be considered as sufficiently severe to render people incapable of competitive employment. The 1970 U.S. Census shows approxi- mately one million persons between the ages of 18 and 64 institutionalized in mental hospitals and nursing homes for the aged (U.S., Department of Commerce, 1973). The residents of nursing homes were not necessarily older people. In fact, they fall within the full spectrum of age categories from 18 through 64.

Concerning the distributions of work disability, Table 2.2 presents those obtained in the Ohio State University survey in relation to the standard demo- graphic characteristics (Nagi 1977). The figures show the clear influence of age and race and the lesser influence of sex on percent disabled. The relations of work disability to education, earnings, and total family income are substantial. The latter two variables can be considered as indicators of the economic impacts of work disability upon individuals and families. Although the proportions change, the relations of work disability to these socio-demographic characteristics main- tain essentially the same pattern across surveys.

Turning now to conditions related to work disability, all surveys with the exception of the U.S. Census gathered information about impairments. Further- more, the Social Security Survey and that of the Ohio State University gathered information on limitations in function. Table 2.3 shows the distributions of selected chronic conditions and limitations of activity as reported by the

---

*The population size used here is based on U.S., Department of Health, Education and Welfare, NCHS 1978).

TABLE 2.2

Work Disability and Other Characteristics of Respondents 18-64 Years of Age (percentage)

Characteristics	No Work Disability	Limited in Work Roles and Activities	Disabled
All Respondents (18-64 years)	89.4	4.4	6.3
Age			
18-44	93.4	2.6	4.0
45-54	87.0	5.2	7.8
55-64	77.9	9.5	12.6
Sex			
Male	90.5	4.2	5.3
Female	88.6	4.4	7.0
Education			
Below 9th grade	76.7	7.9	15.4
9-11	86.1	5.8	8.1
12	91.9	4.1	4.0
13 and above	94.5	2.0	3.5
Respondents' earnings			
Below $2,500	82.2	5.0	12.7
2,500-4,999	92.0	3.6	4.4
5,000-9,999	93.9	4.5	1.7
10,000 and above	95.6	3.5	0.9
Family income			
Below $2,500	64.6	9.3	26.2
2,500-4,999	81.5	6.4	12.1
5,000-9,999	90.6	4.1	5.3
10,000 and above	93.3	3.5	3.2
Race			
White	89.9	4.4	5.7
Black	83.6	4.5	11.9
Other	93.8	3.3	2.9

National Center for Health Statistics for 1974. The distributions indicate that certain types of impairment are more associated with the severity of work disability than others. However, this relationship is far from suggesting that impairments constitute meaningful indicators of disability. Though presented differently, the same conclusions regarding the relations of impairments to disability can be drawn from the results of the 1966 Social Security Survey of Disabled Adults (Table 2.4).

In contrast to impairments, indicators and measures of limitations in function relate more strongly to work disability. Two such indexes were constructed on the basis of data collected in the Ohio State University Survey of 1972: Physical Performance Scale (PPS) and Emotional Performance Scale (EPS) (Nagi 1977). The items used in these scales and the distributions of responses are presented in Table 2.5. Limitations in performance along these two dimensions as measured by these two scales show substantial relations to work disability (Table 2.6), suggesting that limitations in function or capacity constitute more appropriate indicators for disability than do impairments.*

THE IMPACT OF DISABILITY

In reviewing the impact of disability as a problem, the most reasonable vantage point is its influence on the lives of the people most directly affected, that is, those defined as disabled. Since disability can be defined from more than one perspective, our approach will be to consider existing data sources where disability was defined in keeping with our present policy and program concerns. As a result, we will focus on data from the Social Security Administration surveys of the disabled where the program rolls and self-definition in terms of work capacity were used to identify the disabled.

It must be remembered during this brief discussion of the economic and employment impact of disability that the data being reviewed were not collected in an effort to obtain more accurate information on the nature of the problem before adoption of a national policy and passage of the Social Security Disability Insurance program. They were collected well after the program was in operation. The earliest study, limited only to disabled workers under the program, was done in 1960. Hence, use of these data in defining the dimensions of the originally identified problem of disability is suspect, since they are unquestionably influenced by the form and operation of the program. However, the data are useful as an indication of the impact of disability within the present framework.

The SSDI program has grown appreciably over the years, most significantly in the past decade. While there has been some moderation in growth more

---

*While a measure similar to this is used by disability-determining personnel when assessing residual functional capacity, this is only done in evaluating disability when the applicant's impairment does not meet or equal the medical impairment standards.

TABLE 2.3

Percent Distribution of Persons with Limitation of Activity, by Selected Chronic Conditions Causing Limitation, According to Degree of Limitation, United States, 1974

Selected Chronic Condition	All Degrees of Activity Limitation	With Limitation but not in Major Activity	With Limitation in Amount or Kind of Major Activity	Unable to Carry on Major Activity
Tuberculosis, all forms	0.4	*	0.4	0.7
Malignant neoplasms	2.2	1.2	1.9	3.7
Benign and unspecified neoplasms	0.9	0.5	1.0	1.1
Diabetes	4.9	3.7	4.7	6.9
Mental and nervous conditions	5.1	3.7	4.7	7.6
Heart conditions	16.2	7.9	16.6	24.1
Cerebrovascular disease	2.7	0.6	1.6	7.4
Hypertension without heart involvement	6.7	4.8	7.8	6.6
Varicose veins	0.9	0.9	1.2	*
Hemorrhoids	0.3	*	0.3	*
Other conditions of circulatory system	3.9	2.3	3.8	6.0
Chronic bronchitis	1.0	0.7	1.1	1.1
Emphysema	2.8	1.1	2.0	6.3
Asthma, with or without hay fever	4.9	7.9	4.5	2.5
Hay fever, without asthma	0.7	1.5	0.7	*
Chronic sinusitis	0.7	0.7	0.6	0.7
Other conditions of respiratory system	2.1	1.6	1.9	3.0
Peptic ulcer	1.9	1.6	1.8	2.3
Hernia	2.4	1.5	2.6	2.6
Other conditions of digestive system	3.2	1.9	3.3	4.6

Condition				
Diseases of kidney and ureter	1.2	0.7	1.3	1.6
Other conditions of genitourinary system	1.7	1.2	1.9	1.7
Arthritis and rheumatism	15.0	10.3	16.9	15.8
Other musculoskeletal disorders	5.9	5.5	6.8	4.3
Visual impairments	5.9	6.4	4.6	8.1
Hearing impairments	2.4	4.4	1.8	1.7
Paralysis, complete or partial	3.3	2.1	2.3	6.9
Impairments (except paralysis) of back or spine	7.0	7.6	8.0	4.2
Impairments (except paralysis and absence) of upper extremities and shoulders	2.1	2.7	2.1	1.2
Impairments (except paralysis and absence) of lower extremities and hips	6.4	9.4	5.5	5.4
Absence, extremity	1.1	1.2	0.7	1.8
Impairments (except paralysis and absence) other and multiple NEC of limb, back, and trunk	1.9	1.5	1.9	2.3
Special learning disability and mental retardation	2.1	1.2	2.1	2.9
Other impairments	3.1	2.2	2.9	4.4
Diseases of eye and ear	5.0	5.5	4.3	6.0
Old injuries, no residual specified	2.9	2.2	3.2	2.9
Chronic conditions	10.9	10.5	10.7	11.7
Condition not specified				
Old age (65 years and over)	2.7	1.3	2.7	4.2
Other	0.7	0.5	0.8	0.7

Notes: Major activity refers to ability to work, keep house, or engage in school or preschool activities. Percentages may total more than 100 because a person can report more than one condition as a cause of his limitation. Asterisk indicates figure does not meet standards of reliability or precision.

Source: "Limitation of Activity Due to Chronic Conditions, United States, 1974," *Vital and Health Statistics,* Series 10, No. 111 (June 1977), table 3.

TABLE 2.4
Severity of Disability, by Major Disabling Condition, Percentage Distribution of Disabled Adults Aged 18-64, by Severity of Disability, Spring, 1966

Major Disabling Condition and ICD Code*	Number	Severity of Disability (percentage distribution)		
		Severe	Occupational	Secondary Work Limitations
Total	17,753	34.4	28.2	37.4
Musculoskeletal disorders (720-749)	5,492	27.9	33.6	38.4
Arthritis or rheumatism	2,201	34.1	28.3	37.7
Back or spine impairments	1,952	21.5	40.9	37.6
Loss or impairment of limbs	874	23.3	31.1	45.4
Other musculoskeletal conditions	465	34.6	33.3	31.8
Cardiovascular disorders (460-468)	4,408	35.8	28.0	36.3
Heart trouble	2,018	35.7	27.7	36.6
High blood pressure	966	39.4	26.7	34.0
Hemorrhoids	204	24.0	31.4	44.6
Varicose veins	407	17.2	33.4	49.4
Other cardiovascular conditions	813	43.8	26.8	29.5
Respiratory and related disorders (241, 245, 470-529)	1,986	26.6	24.0	49.4
Asthma	677	24.7	31.5	43.9
Other allergies	489	15.5	20.7	63.8
Chronic bronchitis	220	17.3	19.1	63.6
Emphysema	149	55.7	11.4	32.2
Tuberculosis	168	30.4	29.8	39.9
Other respiratory conditions	283	40.3	18.7	41.3

Condition				
Digestive disorders (540-586)	1,284	25.9	34.7	39.3
Hernia or rupture	339	15.0	38.6	46.3
Stomach ulcer	517	20.9	33.8	45.1
Other digestive conditions	428	40.7	32.7	26.6
Urogenital disorders (590-637)	451	37.7	25.5	36.6
Endocrine-metabolic disorders (250-260)	690	35.9	21.0	42.9
Diabetes	487	37.8	19.1	43.1
Thyroid	203	31.5	25.6	42.4
Mental disorders (300-329)	1,114	53.9	24.9	21.1
Mental illness-nervous trouble	902	48.2	27.2	24.5
Mental retardation	212	78.3	15.1	6.6
Nervous system disorders (330-369)	922	63.6	20.2	16.3
Epilepsy	171	56.1	18.7	25.1
Multiple sclerosis	102	38.2	46.1	15.7
Paralysis	184	53.3	21.2	25.5
Stroke	257	69.6	16.3	14.0
Other nervous system conditions	208	83.7	12.5	3.8
Sense organs disorders (370-398)	620	29.0	21.8	49.2
Visual impairments	433	35.8	21.9	42.3
Deafness	187	13.4	21.4	65.2
Neoplasms (199)	301	54.8	23.9	21.3
Other and unspecified conditions	487	36.1	15.6	28.3

*Manual of International Statistical Classification of Diseases, Injuries, and Causes of Death, 7th rev. ed., vol. 1 (Geneva: World Health Organization, 1957).

Source: Lawrence D. Haber, "Epidemiological Factors in Disability: I. Major Disabling Conditions," Social Security Survey of the Disabled, 1966, U.S. Department of Health, Education, and Welfare, SSA Report, no. 6 (February 1969); table 7.

recently, there is still a great deal of concern for the number of disabled workers and dependents receiving benefits. As of June 1979, there were 2,877,485 disabled workers and 1,948,907 dependents in current-payment status. The rate of total benefit payments for workers and their dependents was in excess of $1 billion per month (U.S., Department of Health, Education, and Welfare, Social Security Administration 1979).

As an indication of other programmatic expenditures for the disabled, federal and state payments under the Supplemental Security Income program were made to about 2 million persons in the amount of almost $345 million in June 1979. The overwhelming majority of these people were not eligible for SSDI benefits. The level of funds distributed for income maintenance of the work-disabled under these two major programs provides an indication of the basis for present concerns about efforts to deal with the problem of disability.

TABLE 2.5
Responses to Items Comprising Physical and Emotional Performance Scales
(percentage)

	Degree of Difficulty		
Item	*None*	*Some*	*Great*
Difficulty standing for long periods	64.7	26.7	8.6
Difficulty lifting or carrying weights of approximately ten pounds	80.1	13.7	6.2
Difficulty going up and down stairs	78.6	15.4	5.9
Difficulty walking	84.6	11.5	3.8
Difficulty stooping, bending, or kneeling	73.5	19.7	6.8
Difficulty using hands and fingers	89.6	8.1	2.3
Difficulty reaching with either/or both arms	90.2	7.1	2.7
Nervousness, tension, anxiety, and depression	45.8	40.0	10.1
Trouble getting to sleep and staying asleep	60.5	30.3	9.1
Troubled with hands sweating and feeling damp and clammy	73.8	12.1	14.1
Heart beating hard even when not exercising or working hard	69.3	11.2	19.5
Pains, aches, or swelling in parts of the body	65.1	25.1	9.8
Weakness, tiring easily, no energy	52.6	36.0	11.4
Fainting spells, dizziness, sick feelings	83.2	14.6	2.2
Shortness of breath, trouble breathing even when not exercising or working hard	80.4	14.6	5.0

Source: Saad Z. Nagi, "An Epidemiology of Disability Among Adults in the United States," *Milbank Memorial Fund Quarterly/Health and Society* 54, no. 4 (Fall 1976); table 1.

Disability and Employment

Under the program definition of disability, there is an inability to engage in substantial gainful activity. However, the various surveys of the disabled include a range of severity from a limitation in the amount or kind of work which the individual can perform to a total inability to work. The survey data are based on self-reports. These reports of work limitation are used to classify sample

TABLE 2.6
The Relations of Limitations in Function and Work Disability
(percentage)

Characteristics	No Work Disability	Limited in Work Roles and Activities	Disabled
Limitations in physical performance			
Minimal	95.8	1.7	2.5
Some	74.9	11.9	13.3
Substantial	37.6	31.8	30.6
Severe	8.2	23.9	67.9
Limitations in emotional performance			
Minimal	96.1	1.9	2.0
Some	93.1	3.0	3.9
Substantial	82.2	7.7	10.1
Severe	45.6	18.2	36.2

Source: Saad Z. Nagi, "An Epidemiology of Disability Among Adults in the United States," *Milbank Memorial Fund Quarterly/Health and Society* 54, no. 4 (Fall 1976); table 6.

individuals as to whether and to what extent they are disabled. In essence then, the impact on employment is included in the definition of disability. As a result, we meaningfully can report only the number of persons who were classified as disabled or work-limited based on their survey responses. However, as will be seen in Chapter Four, there appears to be a relationship between self-defined disability and the socioeconomic environment in which the individual lives as this affects job prospects.

In the 1966 SSA Survey of Disabled Adults, a total of 17,753,000 persons in the non-institutionalized population aged 18-64 were defined as disabled. Of these, slightly over 6 million were considered severely disabled, that is, unable to work altogether or to work regularly. While most of these people were not working, 14.5 percent were currently working part time, and 1.7 percent full time. About 9 out of 10 of the males with lesser levels of limitation were in the labor force, with the overwhelming majority working full time (Haber 1968).

In the 1972 SSA Survey of Disabled and Nondisabled Adults the same definitions of disability severity were used, but the population studied was aged 20-64. The survey found 15,550,000 disabled persons, of whom 7.7 million were severely disabled. While the data are handled somewhat differently, making direct comparison of current work status difficult, the percent working relative to severity seems basically consistent between the two surveys (Schechter 1977).

Disability and Income and Earnings

Both the number and percent of the non-institutionalized severely disabled receiving disabled worker benefits under the SSDI program rose appreciably between 1966 and 1972. In 1966, disability benefits* were paid to 847,000 severely disabled adults, or 14 percent of the severely disabled (Haber 1968). In 1972, 18 percent of the severely disabled or approximately 1 million of these persons received disabled worker benefits.

Income of the disabled is closely related to severity. The more severely disabled the individual, the lower the income of the immediate family unit composed of the disabled individual, his or her spouse, and children under 18. Earnings, even in family units with a disabled person, provide most of the individual income in our economy. One-fourth of the income of the severely disabled and three-fourths of the income of the partially disabled came from the earnings of disabled married men themselves. However, as the 1966 survey indicated, "The major economic result of severe disability was loss of earnings and increased dependency on public programs or family support" (Swisher 1971). Because age, sex, and marital status affect earnings and income, the impact was greatest on younger severely disabled nonmarried men and women. The severely disabled, as indicated, were mostly not in the labor force and were more dependent on public income maintenance or the earnings of other family unit members. The major income replacement program for the severely disabled was Social Security. Including all forms of Social Security benefits, that is, disability, retirement, survivors, and dependents, "only one-third received benefits, and it supplied less than one-eighth of all income received" (Swisher 1971, p. 29).

An additional consideration relative to the income of the disabled is commented on by Swisher:

> The low income of the severely disabled was in part attributable to the large proportion of older, poorly educated, and minority race members in the group. Many were from the South and from rural areas, in which

---

*Included are disabled worker and childhood disability beneficiaries. However, between 85 and 90 percent of these were disabled workers.

economic opportunity was relatively restricted and income levels were generally lower than in other parts of the country. For many disabled persons, these additional handicaps were an integral part of disability" (Swisher 1971, p. 29).

Based on the 1966 survey data, 45.4 percent of the family units of the severely disabled had 1965 incomes at or below the poverty level. In the 1972 survey, 37.4 percent of comparable units had income below the poverty level. This compared to 9.5 percent of the nondisabled who were studied in the same survey (Burdette and Frohlich 1977).

The basic relationships between disability and income and earnings found in the 1966 survey also were found in the 1972 survey. However, earnings played a smaller part and public income maintenance a larger part in the income of the disabled in 1971 than in 1965. In part, the explanation for this probably can be found in the differences in economic conditions between the two years. Fewer of the disabled worked in 1971 and twice as many drew unemployment benefits than in 1965 (Burdette and Frohlich 1977). As a final consideration, however, it is interesting to note that for disabled worker beneficiaries these benefits contributed a relatively smaller share of 1971 income than 1965 income. The share of income from earnings rose comparably for this group.

3
THE ESTABLISHMENT OF DISABILITY INSURANCE: POLICY FORMULATION AND PROGRAM DEVELOPMENT

In the first chapter we indicated that our value system places great emphasis upon individual rights and in the belief that they can best be assured if national governmental powers are limited. The essence of this belief was stated by John Locke in his *Second Treatise on Government,* when he emphasized the sanctity of the individual and the corresponding necessity to guarantee individual rights (Barker 1962). Locke was essentially optimistic in his faith in the individual's inherent capacity to obtain the "good life." The natural consequence of this philosophy was to assume that only limited government was necessary in order to prevent the occasional transgressions upon individual rights.

The problem for individualists has been how to achieve limited government in the face of social problems which seem to require governmental intervention. As we noted in Chapter One, anti-collectivists have maintained historically that since most social problems are the result of individual delinquencies government involvement in problem alleviation should be minimal. Reluctant collectivists, on the other hand, have stressed that there are social problems to which society has contributed and that under such circumstances the national government has a major responsibility for problem resolution.

This chapter will emphasize how these two views have existed in counterpoint throughout the history of the disability insurance program and how this situation was affected when the disability insurance program was established, how disability was defined as a social problem, the direction and the nature of the policy formulation debate, and the specifics of the program. Perhaps most importantly we shall suggest that these competing views about disability as a social problem have resulted in a disjointed approach to the problem of disability, one which seeks relief for the disabled through policies reflecting apparently competing philosophies about how to accomplish this task. Throughout this book we will contend that this situation has caused infinite difficulties for the disability insurance program.

THE SOCIAL SECURITY ACT OF 1935: AN ATTEMPT TO AMALGAMATE COMPETING VIEWS ABOUT SOCIAL PROBLEMS

The anti-collectivist's position, that national government involvement in social problem amelioration should be minimal, predominated in this country until the passage of the Social Security Act of 1935. Public welfare was for all practical purposes the responsibility of the states and their local governments. This situation was a reflection of the Elizabethan Poor Laws of 1601, which stressed that "giving relief to those who cannot support themselves or secure aid from relatives, friends, or private philanthropy was a function of local government" (Merriam 1946, pp. 7-8). Consequently, indigents were placed in county "poor" homes, and the sick and the mentally retarded were incarcerated in "institutions." These practices coincided with the position that "since pauperism was a form of social disease and degeneracy . . . the proper role of assistance was . . . to provide minimal help in unattractive circumstances, lest those on relief corrupt both themselves and ultimately other members of society" (Stevens and Stevens 1974).

The policy of providing "indoor aid" continued until it was recognized that the aged poor, the needy child, and the unemployed blind deserved better care. As a result, significant programs of "outdoor" relief were developed by the states, some of which were precedents for the Social Security Act of 1935. By the end of 1934, 28 states had passed old age assistance pension programs which in effect removed the aged poor from the alms houses. By 1935, 27 states provided payments for the blind. State programs for child relief focused on providing aid to the needy widows of dependent children. By 1934, all but three states provided such aid. As a matter of fact, interest in the program for the mothers of needy children was so high that a federal Children's Bureau was created in 1912, which served as a model for the Federal Security Administration, the predecessor to the Department of Health, Education and Welfare (Stevens and Stevens 1974).

The unemployment that prevailed during the Depression of the 1930s constituted a severe challenge to the anti-collectivist's assessment of social problems, since it was obvious that many were in need because jobs were unavailable rather than because of the absence of individual initiative. Under these circumstances reluctant collectivists logically argued for national government intervention to ease the situation. However, anti-collectivists maintained their skepticism about the need for such intervention because of their continued concern that even unemployment was exacerbated by many who simply did not want to work.

Grudgingly, anti-collectivists eventually agreed to national government intervention provided it were clear that initiative had been unrewarded because of circumstances over which the individual had no control. In this circumstance the provision of aid by the national government was considered appropriate if it were distributed through insurance-oriented programs, that is, whereby the potential recipient, through payroll deductions, had contributed to a trust fund from which the benefits were taken. Anti-collectivists considered such programs acceptable since they seemed similar to any private insurance policy where a person is insured against the possibility of a future need and is entitled to benefits if the claim is legitimate.

Reluctant collectivists had been leaders in the effort to persuade anti-collectivists to accept the logic of national social insurance programs. However, they felt that the economic situation and the individualistic value system justified broader national government intervention to alleviate the country's social welfare problems. As a result they advocated aid based on need as well as upon whether the applicant was "insured."

These apparently divergent views regarding welfare programs were ultimately incorporated into the Social Security Act of 1935. Social insurance was represented by the Old Age Benefits program, which eventually became Old Age, Survivor's and Disability Insurance (OASDI). (Survivor's insurance was added in 1939, and Disability Insurance in 1956.) Health insurance for the Aged (Medicare) was added in 1965. Unemployment benefits also were included in the original act as part of the Unemployment Insurance program. In these programs, benefits were allocated as a matter of right because of contributions made by the claimants.

Programs for the needy represented in the passage of such public assistance programs as Aid to Dependent Children (later expanded to Aid to Families with Dependent Children and Aid to Families with Dependent Children with an Unemployed Parent), Aid to the Blind (AB), and Old Age Assistance (OAA) also were part of the original act. Aid to the Permanently and Totally Disabled (APTD) and Medicaid were added in 1950 and 1965, respectively. In 1974, OAA, AB, and APTD were combined into the Supplemental Security Income (SSI) program, whereby a guaranteed minimum income is provided for qualified indigent blind, aged, and disabled applicants. In all of these programs aid was given according to need and regardless of whether individual contributions to the program had been made based on prior work. Consequently, general revenues rather than an earmarked payroll tax under which the recipient had contributed directly to the financial support of the program were used to provide financial support.

Although it is not within the purview of this analysis to chronicle the debate surrounding the approval of these programs, it is important to realize that the anti-collectivists were most anxious to avoid unnecessary national government involvement and to limit benefits to the "qualified" as they defined this term. Reluctant collectivists were less concerned about national government intervention and with severely limiting who should receive aid. As a result, severe and sometimes vitriolic debate occurred over whether the national or state governments ought to administer the programs; whether the programs ought to be self supporting, subsidized by the national government, or funded from state funds; and who should be covered by the various programs.

The Social Security Act of 1935 represents the compromises that were necessary to resolve these differences. Anti-collectivists agreed that the program providing benefits to retirees (and, after 1939, to their survivors) should be administered by the national government. Their acquiescence in national administration was a reflection of their tacit acknowledgment that benefits ought to be determined uniformly and dispensed when people were in need through no fault of their own. There was doubt, however, about whether unemployment resulted from economic dislocation (and, therefore, not the fault of the individual) or from an unwillingness to work (and, therefore, a social problem to which the unemployed had contributed). A consequence of this uncertainty was agreement that unemployment compensation should be administered by the states, albeit under close national supervision, and financed by a complicated tax offset program which in effect encouraged both state and national government funding. Although a basic guarantee was provided by the national government, the amount and duration of benefits were allowed to vary among states.* The public assistance programs (AB, ADC, and OAA) were administered through the technique of the grant-in-aid. This technique reflected the view that although some national government administration and funding was necessary, the primary obligation for social problems to which people had presumably contributed should remain with the states.

The anti-collectivists' concern that the national government limit its involvement in social problem resolution to those most "deserving" has continued throughout the years. APTD was not added until 1950 because of a concern about whether indigent disabled were merely malingerers who were able to work. As we shall see, a similar concern delayed the passage of disability insurance. When AB, OAA, and APTD were combined into the SSI program, federal administration and a basic guaranteed income were provided. Applicants for program benefits are indigents in need of government aid. Nevertheless, those who claim

---

*It should be noted that the pattern of state involvement also was influenced by the existence of a successful program of unemployment insurance and compensation in Wisconsin.

disability benefits must qualify under the same guidelines as established for the Social Security Disability Insurance program. And, as we noted in Chapter Two, the Medicaid program has been established to provide medical aid for indigent needy who may have contributed to their problems, while Medicare is for deserving applicants (those who have worked and are not at fault for their need). However, even here the skepticism about extensive government involvement is apparent. Thus, the Medicare patient is responsible for paying part of his or her hospital costs; physician's care is provided only if the applicant has agreed to payroll deductions for Supplementary Medical Insurance (SMI); and private insurance still constitutes a major basis for paying for medical care costs.

DISABILITY INSURANCE: A CONTINUATION OF THE IDEOLOGICAL DEBATE

It is evident, then, that the Social Security Act represented a significant change in this country's general philosophy toward public welfare since it incorporated the views that national government participation was necessary in order to provide aid to indigent needy and that some deserved benefits since they were not at fault for their predicament. However, as we've noted, passage of the act did not signify the end of the anti-collectivist's perspective. Indeed, advocates of this view continued to exercise vigilance in order to prevent what they considered to be unnecessary national government involvement and the introduction of social insurance programs which resulted in the provision of aid to the needy poor. The struggle associated with the establishment of disability insurance is mute testimony to the intensity of their concerns on these matters.

A disability insurance program is especially prone to arouse anti-collectivists' suspicions. Through this program, the potential recipient insures, by payroll deductions, against the possibility of being unable to work. Consequently, like any insurance program, benefits are allocated as a matter of right to qualified applicants. But it was exactly this issue that caused concern since it is extraordinarily difficult to determine when an applicant is entitled to benefits because an impairment prevents work. Anti-collectivists feared that because of this difficulty benefits might be given indiscriminately, thus converting disability insurance into a public aid program.

The problems associated with determining disability were reflected by the fact that the January 15, 1935, recommendations of the Committee on Economic Security, which served as the basis for the Social Security Act of 1935, failed to mention disability insurance. As the committee's executive director recalled, "the problems of the disabled were never given any real consideration . . . [since] invalidity insurance is the most difficult of all forms of social insurance, and should, therefore, be considered as one of the items to come last in a complete program for economic security" (Goldsborough, Tinsley, and Sternberg 1963).

With the passage of the Social Security Act of 1935, however, attention was focused upon disability insurance. Thus, the Interdepartmental Committee to Coordinate Health and Welfare Activities, appointed by the president in 1937, recommended "the development of social insurance to insure partial replacement of wages during temporary or permanent disability." This was felt necessary because of the "inapplicability of unemployment insurance to protect against loss of income during periods of illness and disability" (Social Security Board 1938). The committee stressed that, since the "administrative problems" for permanent as distinguished from temporary disability were different, the "rate of benefits" should not be equal. A temporary disability was defined as lasting up to 26 weeks, whereas a permanent disability was one where the worker "probably would never be able to enter gainful employment."

Since temporary disability was considered much like temporary unemployment, the committee felt that insurance against such an event could "be patterned after unemployment compensation with repetitive certification of disability by a physician as a procedure analogous to repetitive registration at an unemployment office." A permanent disability, the committee felt, was "more like old age retirement in that the worker leaves the labor market in the same sense as does the aged person." For this reason it recommended that "insurance against permanent disability should be established through liberalization of the Federal Old Age Insurance system so that benefits become payable at any time prior to 65 to qualified workers who become permanently and totally disabled" (U.S., Congress, House 1939a).

Congressional opposition to this proposal was intense and reflected the anti-collectivist position that national government participation in such programs ought to be severely limited. Given this reaction, efforts to obtain congressional approval for disability insurance were abandoned. However, it was agreed that the subject required additional study. As a result the Advisory Council on Social Security was appointed in May 1937 by the Senate Special Committee on Social Security and the Social Security Board. The advisory council was charged with considering the extension of old age insurance to new groups, the addition of a program of survivor's insurance, and "the advisability of extending benefits . . . to persons who become incapacitated prior to age 65" (Goldsborough, Tinsley, and Sternberg 1963, p. 39; Berkowitz 1976, p. 44).

It soon became apparent that the advisory council was unenthusiastic about the idea of a permanent disability insurance program. Members of the council were concerned, given the fact of the Depression during the period of their consideration, that people would file for benefits based on their unemployed status rather than their disability and that the program "had the potential to serve as a major source of income redistribution" (Berkowitz 1976, p. 47).

M. Albert Linton, a member of the advisory council who was also president of Provident Mutual Life Insurance Company, expressed this concern by noting, "If you want to adopt a Machiavellian plan to wreck social security, just put in disability and let it run, especially during a period of depression" (Berkowitz 1976, p. 52). Senator Paul Douglas, an architect of the Social Security system, opted for a public assistance program for the disabled.* He indicated that he "wanted to wait on disability insurance until he had more assurance its many problems could be solved" (Berkowitz 1976, p. 56).

Altmeyer, also a leader in the Social Security movement, worried about whether "the social security system could withstand a massive onslaught of disability claimants." Their concern was that "as soon as people lose their jobs they would put in disability claims" (Berkowitz 1976, p. 53). In an effort to prevent this from occurring, the board focused on a definition of disability that would mean that the "worker was unfit to work for the rest of his life" or until eligible to receive old age benefits (Berkowitz 1976, p. 48). But even with such precautions the board split on whether to establish a permanent disability insurance program (Berkowitz 1976, p. 57).

Given this ambivalence the Social Security Board recommended that the establishment of the program be delayed until "a fairly strict definition" could be adopted and maintained for disability determination. It also recommended that "adequate provisions should be made . . . for vocational rehabilitation" so that the disabled could eventually be returned to the labor force (U.S., Congress, House 1938b, pp. 7-8).

Despite the cautious positions of the Advisory Council and the Social Security Board, Senator Robert F. Wagner introduced a bill to permit states to develop their own disability insurance programs with support from federal grants. In an effort to win support the measure imposed severe penalties on those who became disabled between the ages of 55 and 65 by reducing their benefits to 20 percent. Wagner did this to provide "safeguards" against those who might apply for benefits even though they could work and so that the program would not be "overly expensive" (Berkowitz 1976, p. 57; U.S., Congress, Senate, Committee on Finance 1939). Nevertheless, opponents protested that the plan would place both the states and the medical profession under intimate federal supervision because it required "standard" administrative practices and "uniform" medical procedures for determining whether a disability claim was warranted. There also was concern that the proposal was actually a subterfuge for obtaining a national disability insurance program. As a result the bill was abandoned (U.S., Congress, Senate Committee on Education and Labor Hearings 1939, pp. 130, 165, 354, 926, and *passim*).

---

*A public assistance plan was adopted in 1950 for needy disabled, Aid to the Permanently and Totally Disabled (APTD).

The period of U.S. involvement in World War II was not conducive to substantive alterations in the Social Security Act. As a consequence, no changes were made to it from 1939 to 1946. However, interest in disability insurance continued. In 1943 the Committee on Long-Range Work and Relief Policies of the National Resources Planning Board issued a report which advocated, among other things, "the addition of an insurance system which would provide disability and sickness benefits" (U.S., Congress, House 1943). As a result of this recommendation, the Wagner-Murray-Dingell bill was introduced "to provide an integrated national social insurance system," which would include disability and sickness benefits (Goldsborough, Tinsley, and Sternberg 1963; U.S., Congress, Senate 1963; U.S., Congress, House 1963). In addition the Social Security Board (and its successor, the Social Security Administration) annually recommended the payment of social insurance benefits to permanently and totally disabled persons (Goldsborough, Tinsley, and Sternberg 1963; Social Security Board 1942). However, the recommendations carefully provided "that benefits should be payable only after a six months' waiting period, and if there had been recent and substantial attachment to the labor force resulting in social security coverage" (Goldsborough, Tinsley, and Sternberg 1963). These specifications were made to prevent applicants from attempting to obtain benefits even though they might be capable of work or have had a short-term disability.

In 1946, the Technical Staff of the Ways and Means Committee issued a report recommending that disability insurance be delayed until questions regarding its administration and disability determination could be resolved. It also suggested that disability benefits be provided only to those above age 55 or 60 "so that the program could be inaugurated on a fairly modest scale with a minimum of difficulty" (Goldsborough, Tinsley, and Sternberg 1963).

In 1945 and 1946, the Bureau of Old Age and Survivors Insurance (BOASI) "attempted to satisfy the concern that 'unqualified' people might receive benefits by proposing six specific criteria for determining when a disability entitled an applicant to benefits." The bureau recommended (1) that disability should mean an incapacity for work; (2) that incapacity for work should be measured by the "residual functional earning capacity" remaining to the applicant; (3) that while the amount of residual earning capacity should be determined from carefully prescribed uniform rules and regulations, cases could also be judged individually; (4) that medical, vocational, and other personal considerations be included among the guidelines for determining a disability; (5) that labor market conditions *not* (our underlining) influence entitlement to benefits; and (6) that statutory language be developed to guide the entire process which "should be general enough so that policy details might be left to administrative regulations" (Goldsborough; Tinsley, and Sternberg 1963, pp. 47-48).

The references to incapacity for work and residual functional earning capacities (points 1 and 2) were to emphasize that the program was for people whose impairment was so severe that work was impossible rather than for those with limited impairments. The medical, vocational, and "other" personal considerations were suggested as a basis from which to help formulate criteria for making determinations about the legitimacy of an applicant's claim. The prohibition against considering labor market conditions in disability determination was in support of the view that disability insurance should be a program for those whose impairments prevented work rather than for the unemployed needy. The sixth specification was suggested to encourage the establishment of necessary statutory and administrative guidelines in order to implement the policy of providing benefits only to those too severely impaired to work.

However, congressional opponents to disability insurance were concerned about the specification permitting decisions to be made on a case-by-case basis (point 3). They also opposed allowing vocational and personal considerations to enter into disability determination and encouraging "general" statutory specifications so that administrative regulations could implement legislative intent. From their perspective, these provisions would result in a policy of providing benefits on the basis of need rather than the severity of impairments. Given this opposition the 1946 Social Security amendment again failed to provide for disability benefits.

By the way of emphasizing its concern the Senate Finance Committee followed the same procedure it had adopted in 1937, and appointed an Advisory Council on Social Security to study the issue of disability determination. In its 1948 report the council recommended that any program of disability insurance be state-administered and supported with federal grants (rather than become part of a federal contributory system) and that benefits be given only to the permanently and totally disabled. In addition, the advisory council's detailed prescriptions of the disability-determining process reflected the philosophy that benefits should be made available only when clearly justified. These recommendations were profoundly important to the history of disability insurance and still constitute the basis for the present disability determination process.

The advisory council recommended that:

the definition of disability be "designed to establish a test of disability which will operate as a safeguard against unjustified claims";
"compensable disabilities be restricted to those which can be objectively determined by medical examinations or tests" in order to avoid the problem of claims being made "based on purely subjective symptoms";
"total disability lasting more than six consecutive calendar months should be considered permanent if the disability is diagnosed as likely to be of long-continued and indefinite duration";
"periodic medical examinations, as well as other checks and safeguards . . . be relied upon to discover cases in which the beneficiary has recovered";
the applicant wait six months before receiving benefits since this "would make it very unprofitable for would-be malingers (sic) to give up work and attempt to qualify for benefits";

the "mere duration of a total disability for six months should [not] give rise to an automatic presumption of permanency";

benefits should not be given for "mere physical impairment, loss of strength, disfigurement, or diseased condition which results from illness or accident," but "only if the individual is unable to perform any substantial gainful activity"; and

the regulations governing what constitutes substantial gainful activity should be "strict" (U.S., Congress, Senate 1948).

The advisory council's careful delineation of the disability determining process was instrumental in encouraging the House Ways and Means Committee to recommend a disability insurance amendment to the Social Security Act (H.R. 6000) (Goldsborough, Tinsley, and Sternberg 1963). The committee observed that the program was a "conservative" one, confined to "those wage earners and self-employed persons who had been regular and recent members of the labor force and who can no longer continue gainful work" (U.S., Congress, House, Committee on Ways and Means 1949). However, it recommended that administration of the disability determination process should be the responsibility of the Administrator of the Federal Security Agency (the predecessor to the Secretary of Health, Education, and Welfare).

Although the House approved H.R. 6000, the latter recommendation occasioned warnings that a national disability insurance system was being established and that it was not "the proper function or responsibility of the Federal government . . . to compensate individuals for all types of losses in earning capacity" (U.S., Congress, House, Committee on Ways and Means 1949). The Senate echoed this sentiment by rejecting H.R. 6000 on the grounds that more emphasis needed to be placed upon state involvement in vocational rehabilitation "so that disabled persons may be returned to gainful work whenever possible" (U.S., Congress, Senate 1950). As a consequence, the 1950 amendments to the Social Security Act again failed to provide for a national disability insurance program.

The continued potency of the anti-collectivists during this period is indicated by the approval instead (1950) of a public assistance program which provided aid to permanently and totally disabled needy applicants (APTD). Like other public assistance programs (ADC, AB, and OAA) eligibility for, amount, and duration of benefits were left to the states and/or their local governments. Financing came from state and federal general revenue sources (Title XIV, Social Security Act).

Ironically, support for this program came from a minority report issued by some members of the advisory council. The report cited its disagreement with the recommendations made by the majority of the council in 1948, noting that because of the "subjectivity" of disability determination it would be wiser to place a disability program at the local level where control could be exercised over the program, where only the needy could be aided, and where the "emphasis could be put where it belonged, on restoring the worker to productive employment." A consequence of such a policy would be that "doubtful or fraudulent claims ... would be held to a minimum" (Berkowitz 1976, p. 227).

The American Medical Association (AMA) was quick to indicate its support for the minority report. It observed that governmental aid "should always be administered on a local level" with federal help "when a need can clearly be shown" (Berkowitz 1976, p. 228; and Witte 1962, pp. 70-71). The support of such groups as the AMA, congressional opposition to the 1948 advisory council report, the minority report from members of the advisory council, and ambivalence among key members of the council all contributed to the passage of this public assistance program. Indeed, Altemeyer, one of the council's most prestigious members, recommended the APTD program as a plan which the AMA and the Social Security Administration "could live with" (Berkowitz 1976, p. 231).

In 1952, however, efforts again were made to provide at least a nominal program of national disability insurance through the introduction of a "disability freeze." Under this proposal a long-term disability would not be counted against a worker in the computation of the number of quarters in covered employment necessary for retirement or in determining the average monthly wages on which old age benefits were based. The proposed amendment required that before qualifying for the freeze the individual had to be recently and "substantially" employed and had to have had a disability for at least six consecutive months. The freeze proposal was not a true disability insurance program since it did not provide benefits at the time of disability but upon retirement at age 65, when a recipient would be entitled to full OASI benefits.

Despite its limited nature, the proposed amendment resulted in what by this point became a traditional debate. The major point of controversy in the House again centered on the provision that the administrator of the Federal Security Agency be given the power to make disability determinations (U.S., Congress 1952). As a result the House approved the amendment without reference to who should make disability determinations. In an equally bizarre action, the Senate Finance Committee recommended passage but without provisions for a disability freeze. The result was that the conference committee was faced with a meaningless disability insurance proposal. The last act in this unusual sequence of events occurred when the conference committee recommended inclusion of the disability freeze but only on the condition that disability determinations be made by state agencies and that Congress approve the disability freeze provision. Since approval was not forthcoming, the effort to add disability insurance to the Social Security Act was once more unsuccessful (Goldsborough, Tinsley, and Sternberg 1963).

But the fact that the proposal had reached the conference committee stage in the legislative process indicated a softening in the position of the anti-collectivists about the establishment of a program of national disability insurance.

Thus, despite the confusion surrounding the debate, it was becoming acceptable to contemplate a disability freeze as long as disability was carefully defined and the program's administration was not the exclusive responsibility of the national government. The change in anti-collectivist's philosophy was perhaps best reflected in the statements of President Eisenhower. He suggested that national social insurance programs in fact supported the traditional stress upon individual initiative, self-reliance, and free enterprise since, in requiring contributions from the potential beneficiary, such programs were "a reflection of the American heritage of sturdy self-reliance" (Eisenhower 1960).

Given this change in attitude, it was not surprising that in 1954 the 83rd Congress approved an amendment to the Social Security Act calling for a disability freeze. It was recommended that disability be defined according to the specifications outlined by the 1948 Advisory Council Report and that determinations of disability "be made by state agencies administering vocational rehabilitation" (Goldsborough, Tinsley, and Sternberg 1963; U.S., Congress, House 1954). Once provided with opportunities for vocational rehabilitation, it was felt, the disabled ultimately would be restored "to dignity and spiritual values that go with work" (U.S., Congress, House, Committee on Ways and Means 1954). But of even greater significance to anti-collectivists was that state involvement in the disability determination process and in vocational rehabilitation would have the effect of limiting national government involvement in the program. From their perspective the state's proximity to the individual enabled them to judge more adequately than the central government whether a person was eligible for the freeze (U.S., Congress, House, Committee on Ways and Means 1954).*

However, the disability freeze of 1954 still was not a true disability insurance program. The permanently disabled had to wait until retirement before receiving benefits regardless of when the disability occurred. Because of this, H.R. 7225 (which eventually became Public Law 880, the Social Amendments of 1956) was approved by the House two years later. This measure proposed the payment of monthly cash insurance benefits to disabled workers between the ages of 50 and 65 who were totally and permanently disabled. Total and permanent disability was defined as an inability to engage in any substantial gainful activity by reason of any medically determined physical or mental impairment which could be expected to result in death or to be of long continued or indefinite duration.

Although anti-collectivists had in effect conceded the need for some kind of disability insurance by accepting the disability freeze of 1954, they were not enthusiastic over the prospect of a full disability benefit program, even with the strict specifications for determining disability and the emphasis upon state determination and vocational rehabilitation. This attitude was suggested by the

---

*For additional commentary on the importance of this provision to the welfare heritage proponents, see Campbell (1967), p. 96.

testimony of the secretary of health, education, and welfare before the Senate Finance Committee. He indicated that the Eisenhower administration was opposed to H.R. 7225 because of the difficulties in determining disability and the cost of the program and because aid was already being provided under the program of aid to the permanently and totally disabled. In addition, the secretary suggested that there had not been time to study the effects of the disability freeze on the OASI trust fund and that providing cash benefits to the disabled would reduce "the incentive of some disabled persons toward rehabilitation" (U.S., Congress, Senate 1955). Persuaded by this argument and similar expressions of opposition from members of the Senate, the Senate Finance Committee rejected H.R. 7225 as it pertained to monthly payments for adults between the ages of 50 and 65 (U.S., Congress, Senate 1956).

However, the position of the anti-collectivists had been eroded by over 20 years of debate over the validity of disability insurance and by the acceptance in 1954 of the essential ingredients of disability insurance. Consequently, the Senate overruled the Senate Finance Committee and, by a vote of 47-45, approved the full program of disability benefits (Goldsborough, Tinsley, and Sternberg 1963). As a result of the bill, benefits were paid for the first time to persons between the ages of 50 and 65 who were afflicted with total and permanent disabilities. The program was funded like OASI of which it was a part, that is, from a payroll tax on the wages of employees matched by employers and the earnings of the self-employed. In order to qualify for disability benefits, the bill required the applicant to be fully and currently insured under the OASI program;* to have worked for 20 quarters in covered employment during the 40-quarter period that ended with the quarter in which the disability began; to have a disability that would either result in death or be of long and indefinite duration; and to wait six months before receipt of benefits so as to rule out the possibility of temporary disability. The guidelines for determining what constituted a disability were the same as in the 1954 disability freeze legislation, which

---

*"Fully" and "currently" insured are defined in terms of quarters of coverage in employment covered for Social Security. Until recently, a quarter of coverage was credited for a calendar quarter in which a person was paid $50 or more in wages or had $100 or more of self-employment income or agricultural cash wages. For years in which an individual earned the maximum taxable under Social Security, all four calendar quarters were credited. The Social Security Amendments of 1977 changed the method of crediting quarters of coverage but not their significance in the program. These amendments established a yearly earnings amount for crediting quarters of coverage in line with the start of annual earnings reporting. A person is fully insured if he/she has at least one quarter of coverage for each calendar year since 1950 or the year he/she reached 21, if later, and the start of a disability period. Currently insured status, which was dropped as a requirement for disability in 1958, is attained if a person has at least six quarters of coverage during the 13-quarter period ending before the event for which benefits are claimed (U.S., Department of Health, Education, and Welfare, Social Security Administration 1973).

in turn was based on the 1948 advisory council's specifications. As provided in the 1954 disability freeze, the vocational rehabilitation agencies of the state constituted the basic agency for disability determination. In addition, the legislation required applicants for disability benefits to report to the state vocational rehabilitation agency for possible rehabilitation. The bill specified that monthly payments were to be suspended in the event of noncompliance.

Subsequent to the 1956 amendments establishing the Social Security program of cash benefits for the disabled, there were modifications in the provisions governing the program which extended and liberalized its benefits beyond the periodic increases in the general level of benefits. The Social Security Act had included "offset" provisions for disability insurance which provided that benefits be reduced by the amount of any payment based on impairment from any other federal agency or under any other law, or based on a federal or state workers' compensation program. The benefits were not to be reduced if compensation was based on a service-connected disability. Later amendments specified that the disability insurance benefit was to be reduced because of any workers' compensation benefit by the amount which the combined benefit exceeded the higher of 80 percent of "average current earnings" or the disability insurance benefit itself (U.S., Congress, House 1973).

In 1958, amendments to the Social Security Act provided that benefits be paid to wives, dependent husbands, and children of disability insurance beneficiaries (Schottland 1958). In 1960, the disability insurance program was further liberalized by the abolishment of the requirement that benefits could not be given to anyone under age 50. This provision had been included "as a part of the conservative approach of the 1956 disability benefit provisions" (Mitchell 1960, p. 18). In addition, beneficiaries were permitted to engage in a "trial work period" and still receive benefits. This was instituted "as a means of relieving disabled people of anxiety concerning loss of benefits while they test[ed] their possible ability to work" (Mitchell 1960, p. 19).

The major amendment in 1964 dealing with disability insurance provided that an insured worker could establish the beginning of a period of disability as the date it actually began regardless of the date of application. This permitted receipt of benefits for up to twelve months retroactively. This feature was designed to aid those who did not apply promptly for benefits and therefore suffered loss or diminution of benefits. The amendment prevented this from occurring "by providing that disabled workers may establish the beginning of a period of disability as the date of actual disablement even though the application for benefits [was] filed much later" (Social Security Administration 1965).

Because of the passage of Medicare and Medicaid, the Social Security Amendments of 1965 have been referred to as embodying "the most far-reaching social legislation to be enacted since the original Social Security Act" (Cohen and Ball 1965). However, important changes in disability insurance also resulted from the 1965 amendments. The requirement that benefits could not be given unless a worker's claimed disability was expected to be of "long, continued, and indefinite duration," was changed to specify that an applicant was entitled to benefits if the disability could be expected to result in death, or had continued, or was expected to continue for at least 12 months. The 1965 amendments also provided for a reduced number of quarters of coverage in order to be eligible for disability benefits for the blind under age 31 (Cohen and Ball 1965).

The 1967 amendments reflected the influence of both the reluctant collectivist's and anti-collectivist's view of the appropriate policy for the disability insurance program. Thus, they both provided for extended coverage and restricted the circumstances under which benefits could be given because substantial gainful activity was not possible. The coverage requirements for the blind under age 31 were extended to all disabled. Disabled widows and disabled dependent widowers became eligible for reduced benefits at age 50 (Cohen and Ball 1968).

Anti-collectivists were concerned about the issue of substantial gainful activity because of the decision in *Kerner* v. *Flemming*, which held that "mere theoretical ability to engage in substantial gainful activity is not enough if no reasonable opportunity is available" and that it was necessary to "furnish information as to the employment opportunities . . . or lack of them for plaintiff's skills and limitations" (Dixon 1973, p. 95). For anti-collectivists (and others) this decision meant that disability insurance could be converted "into a limited unemployment compensation program" (Dixon 1973, pp. 19-20). As a consequence of their concern, the 1967 amendments required that benefits could not be given unless it were proven that the applicant was unable to engage in any kind of substantial gainful work existing in the area in which the claimant lived or "in several regions of the country" and without regard to "whether a specific job vacancy exists for him or whether he would be hired if he had applied for work" (Cohen and Ball 1968).

THE RESULT OF THE IDEOLOGICAL STRUGGLE

It is clear that the debate between the proponents of the competing philosophies of individualism left its impression upon the disability insurance program approved in 1956. As we have noted, even with the passage of the Social Security Act, anti-collectivists held to the view that the national government should provide aid only when it was clearly justified. Reluctant collectivists, however, felt that aid was also warranted in more general circumstances according to the needs of the applicant. The disability insurance program occasioned a direct confrontation of these views since the anti-collectivists were convinced that the program was really a public aid program in disguise, especially since disability insurance advocates were not very clear about who should be entitled to benefits.

Thus, even though the Interdepartmental Committee to Coordinate Health and Welfare Activities attempted in 1937 to define the disability insurance program as one for the permanently rather than the temporarily disabled, they obfuscated the insurance premise by suggesting that the need for disability insurance was "to insure partial replacement of wages during temporary *or* permanent disability" (emphasis added) (Social Security Board 1938). To anti-collectivists this was tantamount to recommending another form of unemployment compensation where the determination of disability would be contingent upon whether the applicant was unemployed rather than unemployable because of a disability.

Given this uncertainty about what constituted disability, efforts were made by the disability insurance advocates to make the disability determination process more precise. Yet, when the Bureau of Old Age and Survivor's Insurance attempted to outline such a process, they recommended that determination of the "residual functional earning capacity" left to each claimant should be "judged individually" (Goldsborough, Tinsley, and Sternberg 1963, pp. 47-48). This phrase intensified anti-collectivists' feeling that the disability insurance proposal was really a program for the needy. However, the need for certainty in distinguishing the unemployable from the unemployed may have forced the program into an attempt at greater specificity than is possible given the reality of disability as an economic, social, and health issue or as a measurable entity. Disability may be viewed more appropriately as an individual consideration within guidelines for assessment than as a measurable condition using standard specific objective criteria.

The advisory council's recommendations in 1948 dramatically demonstrated the anti-collectivists' concern that national government programs be devoted only to those who were "worthy" of aid. Thus, the recommendations focused upon preventing "unjustified claims" based on "purely subjective symptoms," emphasized the need for medical examinations in order to verify the seriousness of an impairment, and stressed that regulations for determining what constitutes an impairment so severe that substantial gainful activity was impossible should be "strict." Perhaps the epitome of their concern was the recommendation that applicants wait six months before receiving benefits in order to prevent would-be malingerers from giving up work in order to receive benefits.

But even with these recommendations anti-collectivists were concerned by the absence of a mechanism to encourage beneficiaries to return to the labor market and by the fact that the disability insurance proponents stressed the involvement of the national government in the disability determination process. Consequently, they approved disability insurance only when vocational rehabilitation was made part of the program and only when the basic responsibility for disability determination was given to state vocational rehabilitation agencies. This was done in order to prevent excessive national government involvement, about which reluctant collectivists had been historically concerned. Most importantly, this arrangement was agreed to in order to take advantage of the states' experience in the area of rehabilitation. The hope was that this experience would mean that state agencies would exercise special care in determining who should receive benefits and expedite the return of beneficiares to the labor force.

When the disability insurance program was approved in 1956, therefore, it reflected the deep imprint of the anti-collectivists' concern that national government programs provide aid only to those who were clearly deserving. As a consequence the program was insurance-oriented. People could receive benefits only if they had worked 20 quarters in covered employment during a 40-quarter period that ended with the quarter in which the disability had begun. The claim for benefits had to be legitimate, that is, based on an impairment which would either result in death or be of long and indefinite duration. In order to make certain that a disability was of long-term duration the recipient had to wait six months before getting benefits. The severity of an impairment was to be medically ascertained in order to provide a "scientific" basis for claiming that it prevented substantial gainful activity. Disability determination was assigned to state vocational rehabilitation agencies in order to avoid excessive concentration of national government powers. Vocational rehabilitation was stressed in order to return the disabled to work as quickly as possible. Although not part of the legislative enactment, the rules and regulations for disability determination required a process of 100 percent review by the national government in order to assure that only those qualified received benefits. For the most part, however, subsequent amendments and changes in the rules and regulations for disability determination suggest a weakening of the anti-collectivists' position that disability insurance benefits should be allocated to a carefully restricted clientele of qualified applicants.

Thus, to summarize briefly, in 1958 benefits were provided to dependents of disability beneficiaries. The 1960 amendments permitted beneficiaries to engage in a trial work period without losing their benefits and abolished the requirement that benefits could not be given to anyone under age 50. The 1964 amendments resulted in the possibility of up to 12 months of retroactive benefits. The specification of the "long, continued, and indefinite duration" provision in 1965 as meaning expected to last 12 months or more or result in death can be interpreted as an attack on the anti-collectivists' position, since it may permit applicants with less serious impairments to apply for and receive benefits than those of this viewpoint intended. While the more specific definition usually is viewed as providing an administratively clear standard which is, therefore, less vulnerable to judicial interpretation, this is not the only assessment possible.

The *Kerner* v. *Flemming* decision regarding what constitutes an inability to engage in substantial gainful activity represented such a sharp departure from the accepted policy for disability insurance that Congress amended the Social Security Act in 1967 in order to reassert the position that an applicant's ability to engage in substantial gainful activity should be interpreted strictly.

However, this trend away from the original anti-collectivist policy intent for disability insurance continued through changes in the administrative rules and regulations established for disability detemination. Thus, disability determiners may consider nonmedical factors in assessing whether an impairment is so severe that substantial gainful activity is impossible. The 100 percent preadjudicative review by the Social Security Administration, the national government agency responsible for the program, was reduced to 5 percent in 1972, and then changed to a postadjudicative review. As a result, the Social Security Administration and regional offices now review decisions of state disability determination services only after they have been made.

What we have had, then, is a continuation of the ideological struggle over the appropriate policy for the disability insurance program. As we shall see in the chapters that follow, this situation has resulted in confusion about what direction the program should take.

4

THE RELATIONSHIP BETWEEN DISABILITY
AND SOCIOECONOMIC CONDITIONS

In the preceding two chapters we reviewed some of the background to the problem of disability addressed by the income maintenance approach of the Social Security Disability Insurance program as well as the history of policy and program development. The approach we are taking to analyzing this program is the consistency or match between the underlying problem, the policy formulated to deal with it, and the program developed to implement that policy. In this chapter we will present data on the relationship between the rates of people defining themselves as disabled and applying for disability benefits and the socioeconomic characteristics of the states in which they live. These data are used here to assess the degree to which self-defined disability and disability under the program are vulnerable to economic and social conditions. Our expectation is that the definition of the problem of disability built into the SSDI program, that is, as a personal condition based primarily on the health of the individual, is not consistent with the population's conception of disability or its basis for action with respect to the program. We hypothesize that from this perspective the SSDI program does not deal adequately with the underlying problem of disability and also that the intent of the policy is not well matched by the program because of its emphasis on physical and mental impairment as prima facie evidence of a disability's existence.

SELF-DEFINED DISABILITY AND STATE CHARACTERISTICS

Given the rationale for the ecological analysis discussed earlier, it is reasonable to hypothesize that differences among states or other geographic areas in socioeconomic, demographic, and other respects affect the probability of an individual claiming disability. If there are environmental considerations in becoming disabled and coping with disability, then areas with different characteristics should show different rates of disability and possibly differences in the composition of the disabled population. Disability may be reported more frequently in areas with low median income, low education, and a low percentage of the labor force working in manufacturing than in less "depressed" areas.

If this is the case, a strong argument can be made for dealing with disability primarily as a reflection of the general environmental situation and only secondarily as an individualized health problem. Health condition is unquestionably one factor in the explanation of disability. Our concern here is to assess the importance of area socioeconomic characteristics apart from individual or aggregate medical factors. We expect these characteristics to interact with medically determinable impairment in leading to disability.

The data to be presented here do not include an estimate of the objective health condition of a state's population. No secondary data exist comparing the objective morbidity status of populations in the various states. The comparative state morbidity data that do exist are subjective; based on self-definition and self-report of health conditions, they therefore would not clarify whether state variations in rates of self-defined disability relate to differences in objective health status of the populations. An additional complication is that those data which do exist are not available for all states. A direct state-by-state measure of objective health was beyond the scope of the research reported.

DATA ON SELF-DEFINED DISABILITY FROM THE 1970 CENSUS

Two primary analytic efforts were undertaken in dealing with the data on self-defined disability: assessment of the interrelationships among categories of the disabled and analysis of the impact of socioeconomic characteristics on the explanation of variance in the state-to-state rates.

The percent of self-defined disabled by state in the 1970 U.S. Census of Population ranged from a low of 6.7 to a high of 13.3. For severe disabled, those unable to work altogether, the figures were 1.94 and 7.0. These figures represent sizable differences in the percent disabled within the states. If a large proportion of the variance in percent disabled can be accounted for by area socioeconomic characteristics, then disability possibly can be conceptualized as a socioeconomic consideration. Such a conceptualization would indicate the desirability of reviewing present approaches to dealing with disability.

Undoubtedly, there are impaired persons who would find it impossible to engage in almost any form of substantial gainful activity under any circumstances. However, other people who meet or equal the technical medical impairment listing standards for disability are, in fact, currently employed. There are other

individuals who cannot work because they are functionally limited for performing tasks they once performed and have not been trained to do things their
residual capacities permit them to do. We believe these aspects of the fit between
the individual and the job are in part socioeconomic considerations and affect
the rate of people in a given area who report themselves as disabled or apply for
disability benefits.

This rationale forces us to consider the following possible model of disability in a geographic area. There is a base of potentially self-defined disabled
persons in any area, that is, those with medical impairments. If there are adverse
local economic conditions which make it difficult for persons to enter or remain
in the work force, more people will report themselves as disabled. Under more
favorable economic conditions fewer people will consider themselves disabled.
These differences will show up as higher or lower rates of people who report
themselves as severely disabled relative to the rate who consider themselves
non-disabled.

The rate of people who report themselves as partially disabled will be more
stable across areas because this group serves as a "swing" category between the
non-disabled and the severely disabled. That is, under negative conditions some
persons may consider themselves severely disabled who would report themselves
as partially disabled under more favorable circumstances. Under favorable
economic conditions, persons might define themselves as non-disabled who
might consider themselves at least partially disabled under negative economic
conditions. As a result, the state rate of severe disabled will have a major effect
on the total rate of disability in the state and the rate of partially disabled,
aside from being more stable across states, will be a poor predictor of either the
rate of severely disabled or the total rate of disability in the state.

The data tend to support the conception of the general interrelationships
among categories of the disabled, although possible alternate explanations
cannot be eliminated completely. We anticipate relative stability in the size of
the partially disabled group from state-to-state. The standard deviation of the
mean percent partially disabled within each state was about one-half the
standard deviation of the mean percent severely disabled, although the mean
percent partially disabled was half again higher than the mean percent severely
disabled. The rate of partially disabled appears to be more constant across states
than either of the other rates.

Mean and Standard Deviation for
State Rates of Self-Defined Disability

	$\bar{X}$	S.D.
Partially Disabled	6.04	0.74
Severely Disabled	4.11	1.32
All Disabled	10.14	1.67

The correlations among these three categories of disability showed the rates of severely and partially disabled were correlated at a level (+.25) which explained only 6 percent of their respective variances. The rates of partially disabled and all disabled had r = +.64 accounting for 41 percent of the variance. However, the correlation of +.90 between severely disabled and all disabled explained 81 percent of the variance.

These findings indicate the overall rate of disabled in an area is best predicted from the rate of severely disabled and that the partially and severely disabled rates are not meaningfully interrelated.

Socioeconomic Characteristics Analysis

Our conception specified that under adverse economic conditions there would be a higher percentage of people who considered themselves disabled than under more favorable conditions and that this difference would appear in the percent of people who considered themselves severely disabled.

Ten socioeconomic characteristics variables explained 82 percent of the state-to-state variance in the total percentage of persons who considered themselves disabled (see Table 4.1). The single best predictor variable was the percent of families earning under $4,000, which explained 51 percent of the variance. Of the six variables with F-tests significant at the .05 level or better, two failed to explain variance in the direction predicted. These were the index of occupational

TABLE 4.1

Stepwise Multiple Regression State Self-Defined Disability Rate and Socioeconomic Characteristics

Variable	Beta	F-Test	Multiple R^2
1100 Families earning under $4,000	.9869	37.06[a]	.5100
1121 Self-employed or unpaid family worker	-.7238	28.59[a]	.6026
1103 Families with Social Security income	.3743[a]	18.56[a]	.6996
1120 Occupational diversity	-.2901	5.11[b]	.7477
1113 Unemployment	.1581	2.49	.7715
1107 Males (under 65) in labor force	.3452	5.70[b]	.7927
1108 Females (under 65) in labor force	-.2438	5.05[b]	.8220
1115 Labor force with less than ninth-grade education	-.1016	.54	.8238
1123 Industrial diversity	.0337	.13	.8241
1125 Part-time workers	-.0367	.08	.8245

[a]Significant at .01 level.
[b]Significant at .05 level.

diversity* and the percent of males under 65 in the labor force. Separate analyses of the two levels of disability provide some possible explanations for this situation.

When we look at the area socioeconomic characteristics that explain the interstate variance in the rates of disabled at different levels of severity, it becomes apparent that there is some greater degree of consistency in critical variables and their direction of measurement for the rates of severely disabled and all disabled than between either and the rate of partially disabled.

Table 4.2 shows that for the percent severely disabled the pattern is quite similar to the pattern for total disabled but closer to what was hypothesized. Overall, 88 percent of the variance is explained by our ten socioeconomic variables. Again, the poverty measure is the single best predictor, explaining 45 percent of the variance. Here, the five variables with significant F-tests all relate in the direction hypothesized.

TABLE 4.2

Stepwise Multiple Regression State Self-Defined Severe Disability Rate and Socioeconomic Characteristics

Variable	Beta	F-Test	Multiple R^2
1100 Families earning under $4,000	.6667	25.23[a]	.4476
1121 Self-employed or unpaid family worker	-.5862	27.98[a]	.7196
1103 Families with Social Security income	.3288	21.36[a]	.8106
1108 Females (under 65) in labor force	-.2339	6.93[b]	.8437
1125 Part-time workers	-.2182	4.15[b]	.8647
1123 Industrial diversity	.0350	.21	.8687
1107 Males (under 65) in labor force	.1816	2.35	.8719
1115 Labor force with less than ninth-grade education	.1614	2.05	.8743
1113 Unemployment	.1192	2.11	.8799
1120 Occupational diversity	-.0932	.79	.8823

[a]Significant at .01 level.
[b]Significant at .05 level.

When we look at the effort to explain variance in the rate of self-defined partially disabled (see Table 4.3), we see a different situation. A total of 75 percent of the variance is explained. However, three of the six variables with significant F-tests did not explain variance in the direction predicted. The index

---

*The index of occupational diversity was constructed so that the higher the index score, the lower the diversity.

TABLE 4.3

Stepwise Multiple Regression State Self-Defined Partial Disability Rate and Socioeconomic Characteristics

Variable	Beta	F-Test	Multiple R^2
1120 Occupational diversity	-.4894	10.24[a]	.4356
1115 Labor force with less than ninth-grade education	-.5189	10.01[a]	.4955
1100 Families earning under $4,000	1.0384	28.89[a]	.5896
1103 Families with Social Security income	.2579	6.20[b]	.6382
1121 Self-employed or unpaid family worker	-.5875	13.27[a]	.6732
1125 Part-time workers	.3079	3.90	.6970
1107 Males (under 65) in labor force	.4557	6.99[b]	.7274
1113 Unemployment	.1441	1.45	.7437
1108 Females (under 65) in labor force	-.1326	1.05	.7507
1123 Industrial diversity	.0135	.01	.7508

[a]Significant at .01 level.
[b]Significant at .05 level.

of occupational diversity was the best single predictor explaining 44 percent of the variance, but not in the direction hypothesized. It seems probable that partial disability is conceptually different from severe disability and, therefore, that the rate of such self-definition in the state is subject to different factors. The rate of partially disabled, as indicated, is also more stable from state-to-state.

The two measures of general socioeconomic situation are important predictors in both situations and predict in the same direction for both severe and partial disability. The more negative the general socioeconomic situations, the higher the rates for both levels of disability. The labor force factors of primary importance within the socioeconomic characteristics are very different for the prediction of the two rates.

For the partially disabled, the three variables with significant F-tests that predict in the opposite direction from what was hypothesized are all labor force factors. They indicate that a more positive employment situation is related to a higher rate of self-defined partially disabled. The one additional labor force factor with a significant F-test on the rate of partial disability (percent self-employed or unpaid family worker) predicts in the same direction for the rates of both partially and severely disabled, indicating a negative employment potential is associated with higher rates. The two additional labor force factors with significant F-tests for the rate of severe disability predict in the direction hypothesized, that is, the more negative the employment situation, the higher the rate.

For the severely disabled, there is a very clear pattern of a high rate being predicted by negative socioeconomic conditions and a depressed labor market. For partial disability, only the general socioeconomic measures clearly point to a relationship between negative conditions and a high rate of self-defined partially disabled. With the labor force factors, there is a suggestion of a relationship between more positive characteristics and a higher rate of partially disabled. When this is considered along with the greater state-to-state consistency in the rate of the self-defined partially disabled, it provides an additional indication that the "partially disabled" may be serving as a swing group between the non-disabled and the severely disabled as opportunities for employment vary. The relationships to the state rates of all disabled show the effects of combining two somewhat different concepts of disability into one overall rate.

Analysis Using Disaggregated Categories

As an additional point of analysis, we assessed the value of the socio-economic characteristics in predicting to self-defined disability when using rates that were disaggregated by various other factors of interest. Thus, we looked at the rates of partially, severely, and all disabled within categories of sex, age, race, and years of education. The multiple regressions for the disaggregated groups and the socioeconomic characteristics are included in Appendix C.

The socioeconomic characteristics explained more of the variance for male disability rates than for either the female or combined rates. There is a pattern of a lower level of explanation of variance for the disaggregated rates when the population is categorized by age (under or over 55), race, or educational level. The one exception is for the rate of partially disabled among those with 9-12 years of education.

Less of the variance in all three rates of disability is explained for the 55-and-over group than for those under 55. Similarly, less of the variance in all three rates is explained for blacks than for whites. The overall result from these two pieces of data when combined with the data on explanation of variance by sex indicates a lower level of predictability of disability rates for those groups whose labor force activity is in general more problematic; females, those aged 55 and over, and blacks. With the population divided into three educational levels, it is the group with 13 or more years of education for which there is the lowest level of variance explained. Unlike the situation for sex, age, and race, this is the category where attachment to the labor force is usually more secure. While the percent of variance explained is, in general, lower for the disaggregated categories, this does not mean that this explanation of variance is at a low level. With the exception of the rate of partially disabled among blacks, where the variance explained is 33 percent, this explanation ranges between 52 percent and 90 percent.

The pattern for direction of prediction for those socioeconomic character-istics with F-tests significant at the .05 level or better indicates infrequent differences when the data are disaggregated. However, for rates of disability disaggregated by race, the general economic variables are not significant for the explanation of variance in black rates of disability. The indications are for a greater degree of difficulty in predicting or explaining the variance in rates of black disabled from socioeconomic conditions. This conclusion is similar to the one based on the overall level of explanation of variance for black, female, and over-55 disabled.

Self-Defined Disability and the Never-Worked Population

Because the analysis being performed implies the rate of self-definition of disability relates to the socioeconomic situation, an additional examination was done of the relationship between the various state rates of disability and the percent of people who had never worked. The never-worked population in a state is made up mostly of women who have never worked and young men who have not yet started to work. Two technically different measures of this population were used: those in the general population who have never worked and those not in the labor force who have never worked. However, the two state rates are correlated at +.98.

The rate of partially disabled in the state is correlated at +.13 with both rates of never-worked. The rate of severely disabled, however, has a +.77 correlation with the general population rate of never-worked and a +.81 correlation with the not-in-the-labor-force rate of never-worked.

The interrelationships between the rate of self-defined severely disabled and the rates of never-worked are supportive of a depressed economy and labor market hypothesis explaining state-to-state variation in both these measures. There is a logical basis for speculating on the possibility that both these groups would be larger under more difficult economic conditions and are a response to the problem of getting and holding a job under such circumstances.

Implications for the Nature and Definition of Disability
at the Societal Level

This general conception of the nature of disability and the relationship between state characteristics and the size of the self-defined disabled group suggests that self-defined disability and its aggregate aspect, the state rate, are affected by the ability to obtain and hold a job more so than the ability to obtain and hold a job is affected by the self-defined disability. We anticipate that the rate of self-defined disabled within a state is highly correlated with the rate of application for Social Security Disability Insurance benefits. These two measures of disability have certain conceptual and operational overlaps and certain marked differences.

Conceptually, it is logical to expect a self-definition as disabled before an individual applies for a disability benefit. Even for individuals who did not initially consider themselves disabled, it is difficult to envision the situation in which they would not have come at least tentatively and conditionally to the self-definition as disabled based on the responses and suggestions of others prior to applying for disability benefits. As a result, we basically expect that applicants for SSDI benefits are also self-defined disabled. However, we would expect many self-defined disabled persons, even those who considered themselves severely disabled, that is, unable to work altogether, would not apply for benefits. This could result from various factors: the individual does not identify with the labor force, has no recent work experience or program coverage; there is a lack of familiarity with the program; the disabled person is not a prime earner so the departure from the labor force does not result in economic privation and thus there is low motivation to seek earnings replacement through SSDI benefits; and so on.

Additionally, the individual's application may not be evaluated for a disability determination because he/she is not disability insured, that is, not eligible to receive SSDI benefits. This makes a distinction between self-defined disability and application for SSDI benefits which is significant for the aggregate rate measures used. For applications, we are concerned with the rate of initial determinations as measured against the size of the disability-insured population in the state. For the self-defined disabled, the base is the entire state population age 16-64. Many of those in the state population age 16-64 are not disability-insured; so while applicants are a subgroup of the self-defined disabled, the rates for these population categories are computed against two different bases. What is important conceptually is that before an individual applies for benefits there first must be a self-definition as disabled. If, in addition, the individual is eligible or covered for disability insurance purposes, that is, is disability insured, he/she may apply for SSDI benefits assuming the person is not engaged in substantial gainful activity.

We would expect fewer persons to apply for SSDI benefits than consider themselves disabled and the rate of applications to be lower than the rate of self-defined severely disabled, even taking into account the size differences between the bases. In states with a higher rate of self-defined disability, we expect a higher rate of disability-insured persons to apply for SSDI benefits. We assume the percent of persons in the state who are insured for disability is not related to the rate who are self-defined disabled. We hypothesize that the state rates of self-defined disability and application for SSDI benefits are both related to the same set of state socioeconomic characteristics. Additionally, we hypothesize that the higher the rate of application for SSDI benefits the higher the rate of awards as a percentage of the disability-insured population.

Having analyzed in a general way the relationship between rates of self-defined disability and the socioeconomic characteristics of the state, we will turn our attention in a later section to the relationship between these state characteristics and the rate of application for Social Security Disability Insurance benefits. However, it is appropriate here to assess the relationship between the rate of self-defined severely disabled and the program measure of state rate of application for SSDI benefits.

The rate of self-defined severely disabled is correlated at +.89 with what we have called the application rate. This indicates that the rate at which a state's population defines itself as severely disabled is predictive of the rate of applications the SSDI program will receive. A comparative analysis of the socioeconomic characteristics of geographic areas in terms of their rates of application for and award of Social Security Disability Insurance benefits similar to the assessment for rates of self-defined disability should provide data useful for policy formulation and administration of public and private income maintenance programs for the disabled. These data should be valuable also for disability prevention and rehabilitation programs, by increasing our knowledge of the environmental, extra-individual factors affecting disability. In our use of this material, the data can contribute to our understanding of the nature of the problem of disability and an assessment of whether the conception of disability built into the policy for dealing with it through Social Security is consonant with data on population self-definitions and responses to the program.

THE SSDI PROGRAM AND STATE CHARACTERISTICS

The distinction between impairment and disability takes on more than theoretical significance in analyzing the fit between problem and policy relative to a program of disability benefits because of the orientation toward impairment as the major basis for award of benefits. While this is not the sole standard for determining disability under the SSDI program, there is a prime emphasis on medical determination of impairment. If an impairment meets a prescribed standard, the claim of work disability is accepted prima facie if the individual is not actually working at a level of substantial gainful activity. Basically, this is done without questioning whether unique individual capacities or environmental factors might have made it possible for the applicant to continue working despite the impairment, that is, even though there may be persons with educational and job skills similar to the applicant who are working at a level of substantial gainful activity with medical impairments which meet the listings. Applicants who do not meet the impairment listings but who are work-disabled because of the fit between job demands and individual capacity still can prove they are disabled. However, the criteria under which this is possible can be much more rigorous.

We will discuss here the relationship between the state rate of application for SSDI benefits and the same state socioeconomic characteristics shown earlier to be highly predictive of the rate of self-defined disability. The relationship between the application rate and the rate of allowance of the claim of disability for SSDI benefit award at State Disability Determination Services* is also discussed. As noted earlier, the populations of self-defined disabled and applicants for SSDI benefits are different, with awards a subpopulation of applicants. We are approaching the award of benefits as the final step in a process which runs through a self-definition of disability and application for benefits among the insured population.

State Differences in Disability Rates

There is little question that variations in the rate of disability allowances exist among states. As early as 1960, hearings before the House Ways and Means Committee revealed that in 1957 the proportion of substantive denials of initial applications in state agencies ranged from 23.9 to 63 percent (U.S., Congress, House, Committee on Ways and Means 1960, pp. 255-56). A more recent study by the House Ways and Means Committee concluded that the variations which concerned the Committee in 1960 were still present a decade and one-half later since "state denial rates show a range by state from 30% to 56% in fiscal 1973" (U.S., Congress, House, Committee on Ways and Means 1974, p. 18).

These variations suggest appreciable state-to-state differences in the disability program but do not indicate the basis for these differences. Are the applicant populations different in different states? In low-denial states is there a better quality of applications because the applicants represent a higher concentration of truly disabled persons? Is this because there is a higher rate of disabled persons in low-denial states? Possibly the explanation lies in the way in which the standards for disability determination are applied in the different states. How does the state application rate for benefits affect the disability program? We hope to clarify some of the relationships among various of the disability program measures in the material below as well as to determine how these interact with socioeconomic considerations.

The variations in denial rates were cited by the congressional hearings as an indication of how far state rates of allowance of processed applications strayed from the national allowance average, which was assumed to reflect the acceptable rate as prescribed by the standards of the program. For instance, a comparison of the 1962 denial rates relative to the national average showed that the 29.8-50-percent spread observed was not serious since two-thirds of the states varied from the national average by 5.8 percent or less (Social Security Administration 1962). However, this approach to program monitoring is limited as a basis for determining how well the program is operating because it fails to take into account the effect interstate variations in application rates may have upon disability allowances.

---

*At the time these data were collected, the name used for these offices was Disability Determining Units.

Concern was expressed in the same report about the apparent relationship between application rates and claimants' economic needs; it was feared that this relationship affected the denial rates. The specific concern was that the conditions that result in applications for disability benefits are not spread uniformly throughout the United States. A 1969 Social Security report seems to confirm this observation, noting that high denial rates occurred in areas where there was an absence of "selectivity" in taking claims and when the "service area characteristics" consisted of high illiteracy, high unemployment, and a high percent of minority population (Social Security Administration 1969).

FACTORS PREDICTING RATE OF APPLICATIONS

The issue first becomes one of determining the validity of the assumptions about the relationship between socioeconomic characteristics and the rate of disability applications. For this, the same multiple regression technique and the same state socioeconomic characteristics were used as with the rates of self-defined disability.

These data in Table 4.4 indicate that 78 percent of the variation among states in the rate of application comes from nine of the ten socioeconomic characteristics used in the analysis, with only the percent of persons in the labor force with less than a ninth-grade education making no contribution to the

TABLE 4.4

Stepwise Multiple Regression SSDI Application (Initial Determination) Rate per Disability-Insured Population and Socioeconomic Characteristics

Variable	Beta	F-Test	Multiple R^2
1100 Families earning under $4,000	.6489	14.76[a]	.4887
1121 Self-employed or unpaid family worker	-.4291	8.40[b]	.6239
1108 Females (under 65) in labor force	-.2778	5.53[b]	.6986
1103 Families with Social Security income	.3429	12.38[a]	.7647
1125 Part-time workers	-.1989	2.17	.7729
1113 Unemployment	.1232	1.51	.7798
1107 Males (under 65) in labor force	.0625	.19	.7813
1120 Occupational diversity	-.0706	.25	.7821
1123 Industrial diversity	.0356	.16	.7829

Note: Variable 1115, percent of labor force with less than a ninth-grade education, non-disabled, does not appear in the table because it did not reach the minimum F-level for inclusion in the stepwise multiple regression.

[a]Significant at .01 level.
[b]Significant at .05 level.

explanation of variance. Four of these nine characteristics had significant F-tests, influenced the rate of applications in the directions hypothesized, and explained 76 percent of the variance. These are: percent of families with less than $4,000 income, percent self-employed, percent of females under 65 in the labor force, and percent with SSA income. These four variables also were the most significant in explaining the rate of self-defined severe disabled in the state, as discussed earlier. It is of interest to note especially that the single best predictor in both cases is the approximation to a poverty rate among the non-disabled residents of a state, that is, the percent of families earning under $4,000 for the year. This one factor explained 45 percent of the variance in the rate of self-defined severe disabled and 49 percent of the variance in the rate of application for SSDI benefits. The remaining five socioeconomic variables in the analysis did not show significant F-tests at the five-percent level.

Thus, the rate of disablity benefit applications was higher if the percent of non-disabled in poverty and on SSA benefits in a state was high and if the level of self-employment and percent of females under 65 in the labor force were low. In short, these unfavorable economic and social conditions can be interpreted as tending to encourage applications for benefits, as well as self-defined disability. We will have more to say later on the implications of these findings as related to the definition of disability incorporated into the policy underlying the SSDI program. Suffice it to say at this point that the aggregate population basis for self-definition and entry into the program seems highly associated with social and economic factors. This does not dispute the probable existence of medically definable impairments within the populations of persons who define themselves as disabled and apply for benefits. It does raise questions as to the relative importance of the impairment in the self-definition and application for at least a segment of the "disabled" population and, hence, on the heavy reliance on medical impairment in the program's concept and administration.

Given this relationship, which shows that a substantial portion of the interstate variation in SSDI application rates is explained by aggregate socioeconomic factors indicative of need and a depressed economy, the next question of concern is the relationship between application rates and rates of award of SSDI benefits.

THE RELATIONSHIP BETWEEN SSDI APPLICATION AND AWARD RATES

The potential impact of the rate of applications on disability awards also concerns personnel in the state Disability Determination Services (DDS) and those involved with the disability program within the various Social Security regional offices.* For instance, one disability determination unit director in the East suggested that the number of applications had risen in that state because of the elimination of the requirement that a disability had to be of "long, continued, and indefinite duration," since this resulted in applications from claimants with doubtful disabilities and who were in financial need. Another Eastern state director indicated that more applications from the unemployed had influenced disability benefit determinations. Personnel in a Midwestern regional office suggested that variations in disability benefits were influenced by prevailing state attitudes toward the provision of welfare. They maintained that those states which were hostile toward the provision of welfare tended to discourage applications. Consequently, the percent of denials was lower than in states with more hospitable attitudes and, therefore, higher application rates. Personnel within another region offered similar observations and agreed that high denial rates could well be the result of a tacit policy of accepting applications regardless of the nature of the claimant's disability. Additionally, it was suggested that variations in denial rates could result from state officials encouraging applicants to apply for the federally funded disability benefits rather than for state-funded assistance programs. Discussions with personnel from one of the Southern regions, and with a variety of officials from a Southern state disability determining unit, resulted in similar suggestions that higher award rates could be a function of the large number of applicants resulting from a policy of encouraging the needy to apply for disability insurance benefits in order to lighten the load on state programs. Specific reference also was made to the high number of applications for disability benefits in states with significant percentages of poor persons and unskilled labor with minimal education.

The implications from this review are that interstate variation in disability awards may indeed be closely related to differences in application rates. Given this possible relationship, one cannot evaluate state allowance rates meaningfully without taking into account the rate of applications from the disability-insured population.

For this reason, the measure of rate of awards used was computed using the disability-insured population as the base for the ratio. This measure is roughly equivalent to the insurance company concept of the percentage of policy holders who have claims paid. The denominator of the equation can be considered equivalent to the number of persons with a given type of insurance coverage. In any given year, only a small percentage of these people may have

---

*This information results from interviews conducted from July 8, 1974, to July 30, 1974. Information was obtained from officials in six state disability determining units and four federal regional disability insurance offices. State DDS directors, supervisors, and, whenever possible, disability determination examiners were interviewed in the state agencies. In each of the regional offices, the representative of the Disability Insurance program was interviewed when available.

sustained a loss related to the risk covered by the insurance. Of the population with such a basis for a claim, only a small percentage may apply for any benefit or recovery. Only a small percentage of the "insured for disability" population will consider themselves disabled severely enough to justify applying for benefits. Just as an insurance company will disallow claims it considers unwarranted, so the disability determination process is supposed to deny claims for disability benefits considered unsubstantiated.

If the rate of claim applications submitted was consistent over time and from area to area, monitoring the rate of allowance for those applications received would provide a basis for control over expenditures for claims or benefits. This is the point of studies comparing variations in rates of allowances to a national allowance average. But if the rate of insured persons who file claims is three times higher in some states than others, then using a standard percent of applications approved as a guideline for a claims-processing review could result in a massive drain on resources from states with high application rates. If there were more insurance-related losses in some states than in others, that is, if a state had a higher rate of application for disability benefits based on objective individual considerations, such as more impairment, illness, or injury, or more inability to engage in substantial gainful activity, such a higher rate of insured persons having claims approved would be justified. However, if this were not the case and the applications were the result of other factors, for instance, claims based on a need for money, then applying the same standard for percent of applications approved would not be appropriate. It would result in an unjustified higher rate of awards to insured, that is, more insured persons having claims paid, and would exceed actuarial predictions, resulting in a deficit for the program.

The use in our analysis of the rate of awards per the population insured for disability* permits an assessment of the combined effect of differences in the application rate and rate of processed applications that are approved. It permits us to analyze for the effect of other variables on the combined effect. Tables 4.5 and 4.6 present the basic distributions of the 1970 application and award data used to compute rates in this manner.

Table 4.5 suggests that awards as a rate per disability-insured vary considerably from state to state. This is seen most clearly in the range in award rates between the lowest and highest award states and in comparing each to the mean. They indicate that although as a mean for all states approximately 0.5 percent of

---

*Comparing the number of awards to the number of persons covered by disability insurance in effect combines the application rate per insured population with the rate of approval of applications received. The interaction of these two variables is the product of multiplying the application rate by the award rate. This results in the rate of award per population insured for disability as indicated in the following formula:

applications/insured for disability x awards/applications
= awards/insured for disability

TABLE 4.5
Awards per 100,000 Disability-Insured Population, 1970

Awards	Number
Lowest state	199
Highest state	1,031
Mean for all states	470
Standard deviation	110

TABLE 4.6
Applications per 100,000 Disability-Insured Population, 1970

Applications	Number
Lowest state	440
Highest state	1,774
Mean for all states	1,001
Standard deviation	286

the disability-insured were awarded benefits, less than 0.2 percent received benefits in the lowest award rate state, compared to over 1 percent in the highest award rate state.

Table 4.6 indicates that this wide variation in awards is matched by the fluctuations in applications from the disability-insured. This is implicit in the great disparity between the lowest and highest state application rates per 100,000 disability-insured population. Although the mean percent applying in each state was slightly over 1 percent of the insured population, less than 0.5 percent applied from the lowest application rate state compared to just under 2 percent in the highest application rate state.

The correlation between application rate and award rate per disability-insured population was +.92. On the other hand, the percent of processed applications allowed decreased as the application rate increased (-.42). This relationship indicates that a high application rate results in a lower percent of the applications processed being approved. However, this relationship is much weaker and indicates far less program impact than the effect of a high application rate on the percent of disability-insured persons who are awarded benefits. The indications are that higher application rates may result in some tightening of review procedures or possibly that they bring in a somewhat higher percent of claims that cannot qualify. In any event, they bring in many more, in absolute terms, that do qualify or, at least, are awarded.

These findings dramatically indicate a great interstate variation in award rates that is closely related to large interstate variation in the rate of applications from the disability-insured population. The dependence of award rates on applications has important implications for the actuarial projections for disability insurance. The overall program rate of applications is higher than it was in an earlier period. While the data presented here do not bear on this issue, it is an important consideration to keep in mind.

THE FIT BETWEEN PROBLEM AND POLICY

A basic unresolved question is whether the higher rate of awards in high application rate states relates to more of these applicants meeting the objective standards for determining disability or is the result of the allowance of benefits based on economic considerations. If the first explanation is correct, then, although there are actuarial implications, the program is functioning as designed, to provide benefits to claimants who cannot engage in substantial gainful activity because of the nature of a disability. If, however, benefits are provided on the basis of economic factors, then the situation is more serious because it suggests that the program's emphasis is not on the insurance premise, upon which it was founded, but on need as the paramount consideration.

The data presented here suggest that varying application and disability award rates are related to the socioeconomic characteristics of a state's population. This fact in itself does not demonstrate violation of the spirit of the disability insurance program, since some aggregate socioeconomic factors can be expected to influence legitimately the rate of award of benefits because they suggest higher rates of disabled persons. For example, the age distribution of a state's population should affect the awarding of disability benefits, especially in view of the assumption that older persons are more susceptible to medical impairments than the young and also are more likely to be disabled by them, that is, are less likely to be able to engage in substantial gainful activity. The program was designed originally to provide disability benefits only to persons between the ages of 50 and 65 based on this situation. This contention has been substantiated by studies which have found that disability recipients tend to fall within higher age brackets (Goff 1973, table 3, p. 7; Brehm 1970).

The distribution by years of education completed by a state's population and its racial and ethnic composition are less obviously related to whether applicants are entitled to benefits. However, disability examiners may consider educational level when reviewing a claim for benefits. The assumption is that claimants with low education will be less likely to overcome even a less severe impairment and engage in substantial gainful activity because the probability is greater that they will be unskilled. Some studies suggest that disability beneficiaries do tend to be persons with lower educational levels (Brehm 1970; Allan and Cinsky 1972). However, it is unclear whether in such instances disability benefits were awarded because the severity of the impairment, when combined with lower educational level, made the applicants unable to engage in substantial gainful activity or whether benefits were awarded because, in view of educational level, claimants could not be expected to obtain employment under the existing economic conditions. This distinction is fundamental since, if the latter is the case, then education has become an economic need factor.

It can be argued that race and ethnicity relate to disability not only because these characteristics are associated with educational level but because certain combinations of these factors suggest such applicants have been employed in more physically demanding jobs, where there is a greater likelihood of severe injuries justifying disability benefits. Studies seem to support the assumption that nonwhites and other minorities account for a disproportionate percentage of disability beneficiaries (Goff 1973, table 3, p. 7; Goff 1971; Brehm 1970, p. 27). But again, it is unclear whether benefits were awarded because of an inability to engage in substantial gainful activity or because people with such characteristics found few opportunities for employment. As with education, if the latter is true, then there is the suggestion that benefits are being provided on the basis of need.

However, aside from factors which indicate a high percentage of older, lower educated, unskilled workers, that is, individual characteristics which can be taken into consideration in the disability determination process, other aggregate state socioeconomic characteristics should *not* relate to the award of disability benefits. The SSDI program was not designed to provide benefits because of general economic conditions and a depressed labor market. Only if the individual applicant's disability were so severe that substantial gainful activity was impossible were benefits to be provided. Indeed, as we have indicated, the 1967 amendments specifically stated that benefits were not to be given merely because a person was unable to find employment in his area of residence. This amendment was in reaction to court cases which seemed to some to permit benefits because employment was not available. The administrative regulations emanating from the Social Security Administration specifically prohibit examiners from giving benefits based on the lack of availability of local sources for employment.

However, in spite of this emphasis, socioeconomic variables do explain a major portion of the state-to-state variance in disability benefit application rates and through this mechanism are closely related to the award rate. Evidence exists, therefore, that the disability insurance program is strongly, if indirectly, influenced by need factors. If need or the limitations of a depressed job market to provide employment opportunities are taken directly into consideration, this is inappropriate under the SSDI program guidelines. However, an "automatic" program response to the pressure of a high rate of applications potentially motivated by general socioeconomic considerations from persons who do meet the standards for award still indicates serious conceptual difficulties within the program. These conceptual difficulties seem to be in the fit between the problem of disability and the policy formulated to deal with it.

In attempting to deal with disability as a social problem, the formulators of policy defined it as an individual's inability to engage in substantial gainful activity because of a medically determinable impairment. The approach taken to dealing with the problem was through the provision of cash benefits to replace, in part, the wages lost because of the loss of work capacity. However, the population basis for both self-defined disability and application for benefits under the program implies a heavy emphasis on the socioeconomic circumstances of the environment in which the individual lives.

The program moved further away from the intended conception of disability in attempting to implement the policy by effectively defining medically determinable impairment as the equivalent of disability rather than as the required explanation for an "inability to engage in substantial gainful activity." This program emphasis established the situation in which persons with a medically determinable severe disability but with compensating abilities could qualify for benefits if other factors made getting or holding a job difficult. As a result, the policy intent of providing cash benefits for those who could not work because of their health was subtly changed by the program to provide availability of cash benefits to those not able to obtain or hold employment who also had a serious health condition, even if that condition were not necessarily the primary reason for the inability to engage in substantial gainful activity. When added to the distance between the population's disability self-definition and basis for action and the policy conception of disability as only those inabilities to work resulting from impaired health, the implications for the ultimate program are indeed serious. But these considerations do not resolve the issue of whether high rates of applications lead to high rates of awards because there are many technically eligible persons available to apply in negative economic circumstances or because these negative economic circumstances are considered in the determination process even though the regulations indicate they should not be. What we have presented indicates only the program's vulnerability and the potential for misuse based on the lack of fit between the underlying problem, the policy, and the program.

5
THE ADMINISTRATION OF DISABILITY DETERMINATION AND FEDERAL-STATE RELATIONSHIPS

A major objective of administrative decision making is to implement programs according to legislative intent. Throughout the debate over the establishment of the disability insurance program it was clear that this intent was to define the problem of disability as an inability to work among people with a work history who had become so severely impaired that substantial gainful activity was impossible. Those with less than severe impairments who were in poverty and/or unemployed for other reasons were not considered part of the disabled population in terms of this policy and program definition of the problem. It is apparent Congress intended disability insurance benefits for the severely impaired worker rather than for those whose primary problem was the need for employment or financial assistance.

However, the data presented in the previous chapter suggest disability benefits possibly have been approved on the basis of labor market conditions and need factors. There is, in any event, a strong association between socioeconomic characteristics and application and award rates. Given the possibility of more direct consideration of these issues it would be reasonable to speculate whether the administrative decision-making process may have been instrumental in altering legislative intent.

Unfortunately, the data on how decisions are actually made within the separate state Disability Determination Services are inadequate for investigating this issue. We can, however, review some related considerations and assess data on the relationship between various characteristics of the decision-making structure in the states and award rates. In assessing these data, we will be particularly concerned with the potential impact of highly qualified disability-determining personnel, in other words, agency professionalism, upon decision-making regarding the receipt of disability benefits.

LEGISLATIVE INTENT

The original intent of Congress was that only those who had worked and were now unable to engage in any substantial gainful activity because of health impairments should receive disability benefits. This policy was fundamental to the anti-collectivists, who were concerned that without such a policy disability insurance might be converted into a program for the unemployed or for those in financial need. Indeed, fear that this might happen led to the statutory provision for state disability determination, albeit with close federal supervision. The anti-collectivists had more faith in the states abiding by legislative intent for the program than they had in the national government.

As discussed earlier, the 1956 amendments contained other specifications designed to enforce compliance with the legislative objective that only severely impaired ex-workers receive benefits. Thus, for example, medical judgment about whether an impairment was indeed incapacitating was stressed. Perhaps the most dramatic evidence of congressional desire to enforce its goal of providing benefits only under carefully prescribed conditions was the specification that a disability had to result in death or be of long and indefinite duration (later changed to expected to last 12 months or more). This provision was designed to prevent applicants from receiving benefits for reasons other than a severe and basically permanent disability. In order to make certain that even such an impairment was not "temporary," applicants had to wait six months before receipt of benefits.

If the legislative intent incorporated in these provisions had continued, there would have been little doubt that the goals of the program were indeed designed to provide benefits only to a carefully determined universe of the disabled population. In fact, however, the incremental changes to the original act of 1956 reviewed in Chapter Three indicate uncertainty about congressional commitment to the original legislative intent. These amendments significantly expanded and liberalized the disability insurance program. This situation has affected the administrative guidelines established for implementing legislative intent as well as the decisions made regarding who receives benefits.

LEGISLATIVE INTENT AND THE ADMINISTRATIVE GUIDELINES FOR DISABILITY DETERMINATION

The administrative guidelines for disability determination have been carefully and copiously prescribed by the Social Security Administration. These rules and regulations have been incorporated into a constantly revised and voluminous Disability Insurance State Manual (DISM), which is distributed to pertinent Disability Determination Service personnel. The point of this procedure is to implement legislative intent by assuring that "uniform adjudicative results" and "evaluation standards" are applied in determining entitlement to benefits.

The guidelines were designed to make certain that benefits were given only for disabilities that prevented the applicant from engaging in substantial gainful activity and which were based on impairments that could be determined medically. This emphasis was designed to enforce congressional intent in line with the recommendations of the 1948 Advisory Council to the Senate Finance Committee. In order to implement this philosophy, a listing of impairments was adopted as the fundamental guide for determining the legitimacy of a claim for disability benefits. These listings specify impairments which in the judgment of the medical community are such that substantial gainful activity is unlikely and which are expected to result in death or last for a continuous period of not less than 12 months. The listings consist of 13 sections of impairments, ranging from ailments afflicting the musculoskeletal system to malignancies. They are incorporated into a pamphlet for use by state Disability Determination Service personnel (U.S., Department of Health, Education, and Welfare, Social Security Administration 1976).

But what of applicants who claimed that they were unable to work even though their impairments were not included in the listing? Such claims introduced an element of subjectivity about the nature of the impairments and, therefore, the possibility that these applicants might not be work-disabled. Given this prospect and the sentiment that such applicants should be rejected, the case could have been made for insisting that impairments had to meet the listings before benefits could be awarded. However, this was not done. Instead, it was agreed that such claims might be legitimate. In order to establish the most rigid administrative standards possible under such circumstances, two techniques were employed: a measure of the residual functional capacity left to an applicant and a sequential process of decision making for disability determination.

Measuring residual functional capacity assumes that disability can be ascertained by establishing an applicant's ability to function despite an impairment. If it is discovered that an impairment has limited effect upon the ability to function, the applicant should be able to engage in substantial gainful activity and not be entitled to benefits. As Figure 5.1 indicates, great care is taken generally to establish precise "measurements" for determining the range of residual functional capacity left to an applicant. The hope is that such precision will diminish the area of subjectivity inherent to such applications.* However,

---

*This figure was obtained as a result of an interview with disability determination personnel in the Oakland office of the California Disability Determination Service.

FIGURE 5.1
Guidelines for Identifying the Range of Residual Functional Capacity

A. Very heavy
    Standing/walking at least 6 hours/8-hour day; lifting in excess of 100 lbs.
    with frequent lifting of 50 lbs. or more.
B. Heavy
    Standing/walking at least 6 hours/8-hour day; lifting 100 lbs. maximum
    with frequent lifting of up to 50 lbs.
C. Medium
    Stand/walking at least 6 hours/8-hour day; lifting 50 lbs. maximum with
    frequent lifting/carrying of up to 25 lbs.
D. Light (Full or Wide Range)
    1. Standing/walking at least 6 hours /8-hour day.
    2. Sitting at least 6 hours/8-hour day using hands or feet for pushing and
        pulling arm and leg controls.
    3. Lifting 20 lbs. maximum with frequent lifting of up to 10 lbs.
E. Narrow Range of Light Work
    1. Restriction on amount of standing/walking (less than 6 hours).
    2. Lifting from 50 to 100 lbs. in a seated position only.
    3. Loss, or loss of use, of one upper extremity.
    4. Significant loss of use of 2 upper extremities.
    5. Inability to lift at least 20 lbs. occasionally.
    6. Inability to lift 10 lbs. frequently.
F. Sedentary
    1. Sitting at least 6 hours/8-hour day.
    2. Certain amount of walking and standing.
    3. Frequent light lifting/carrying of small items.
    4. Maximum lifting of up to 10 lbs.
G. Less than the Full Range of Sedentary
    1. Use of one leg only and have to use a cane (or other assisted ambulation).
    2. Restricted from carrying small objects.
    3. Does not have full use of upper extremities (and restricted to work in
        a seated position).
    4. Can do work as long as alternating sitting and standing i.e., cannot sit
        at least 6 hours/8-hour day.

whatever precision is gained by such detailed specifications is largely diminished by other guidelines which indicate that an applicant's age, education, and previous employment are mitigating factors in disability and also should be taken into consideration.

The purpose of the sequential evaluation process for disability determination is also to limit the amount of subjectivity about whether applicants with impairments that do not appear in the listings qualify for disability benefits. The process incorporates the principles of disability determination in a series of decision-making steps. These steps range from clear-cut instances of disability to those in which judgment plays a crucial role. As Robert Dixon explains, "The tests are successive in the sense that they set forth a progression from 'hard core' disability to 'borderline disability,' and a determiner cannot reach a conclusion until he has considered all the tests" (Dixon 1973, p. 54).

As Figure 5.2 suggests, the first step in the process is to determine whether, on the basis of medical evidence only, an applicant with a severe disability is entitled to benefits. As indicated, benefits are allowed under Regulation A1-1502(a)* if the disability will result in death or last at least 12 months and meets any of the listings specified in the *Handbook for Physicians*. Benefits also may be given for medical reasons under B1-1502(a) if it is determined that a disability is "equivalent" or "equal to" the specific listings in the handbook.

More difficult to determine are cases when an applicant's impairment is not specified in the listings or not considered equal to the listed impairments. Under such circumstances the disability determiner must judge whether the applicant has the residual functional capacity to engage in substantial gainful activity. As previously indicated, although such a decision is supposed to be based on carefully specified standards, age, education, and previous employment may also be considered.

The least difficult decision, given this situation, occurs when the applicant is elderly, has limited education (usually less than sixth-grade), is unskilled, and has been engaged in arduous labor for a substantial period of time (usually 35 years or more). Regulation D1-1502(c) requires the awarding of benefits to such applicants because it is assumed that they are unlikely to obtain substantial gainful activity based on their previous occupation and will be difficult to train for other kinds of employment.

The most difficult decision for the disability determiner is when an applicant claims that an impairment prohibits substantial gainful activity even though it does not meet the listings, is not equal to the listings, and the applicant does not have the characteristics that would permit the granting of disability benefits under D1-1502(c). Regulation C1-1502(b) attempts to provide for uniform

---

*These regulations are specified in "Disability Regulations" in *Code of Federal Regulations,* Title 20, 404.1502, "Evaluation of Disability Except for Purposes of Statutory Blindness or Widow's or Widower's Benefits."

FIGURE 5.2
Sequential Evaluation

I. Severe Disability (on the basis of *medical evidence* only)			
1. Will disability last 12 months or result in death?	No	Not under a disability	
	Yes		
2. Does it *meet* listing?	Yes	Under a disability	A1-1502(a)
	No		
3. Does it *equal* listing?	Yes	Under a disability	B1-1502(a)
	No		
II. Non-Severe Disability (on the basis of *medical evidence* plus vocational factors)			
1. Is this an older claimant who is unable to do customary arduous, unskilled work?	Yes	Under a disability	D1-1502(c)
	No		
2. Does the non-severe impairment of a claimant unable to do *usual* work, in combination with age, education, and work experience preclude other substantial gainful activity?	No	Not under a disability	
	Yes	Under a disability	C1-1502(b)

93

Source: This chart is an abbreviated and modified version of one included in "Sequential Evaluation Process in the Adjudication of Disability Claims." Regional SSA Program Circular, D.F. no. 72-11-C49, S.F. 12/6/72. U.S., Department of Health, Education, and Welfare, Social Security Administration.

decisions in such circumstances by specifying that if a claimant cannot do his usual work benefits are to be granted only if age, education, and work experience preclude other substantial gainful activity in the applicant's region of employment or "in several regions of the country." Furthermore, the decision is to be made regardless of whether a specific job vacancy exists or whether the applicant would be hired. These specifications obviously were designed to prevent applicants from obtaining disability benefits because they are unable to find employment.*

Information indicating the percentage of allowances and denials in each of the sequential stages is difficult to obtain. Dixon estimates that 45 to 50 percent of all cases (applications) are allowed based on the conclusion that the applicant's disability either meets or equals the listings; that 2 to 3 percent are allowed based on the judgment that an applicant's age, skills, education, and previous employment in arduous labor makes substantial gainful activity unlikely; and, that from 8 to 10 percent are allowed in the borderline cases covered under Regulation C1-1502(b). The remaining 35 to 40 percent are estimated to be denials. Dixon suggests that 10 percent of the denials are borderline decisions and that consequently approximately 20 percent of all cases decided fall within the borderline provisions of C1-1502(b). Figure 5.3, which reflects the percentage of allowances and denials for each stage of the sequential process in one region, tends to substantiate Dixon's estimates.

ADMINISTRATIVE JUDGMENT AND THE
DISABILITY DETERMINATION PROCESS

It is apparent, then, that considerable room for administrative judgment remains within the provisions of the sequential analysis despite the efforts to reduce subjectivity as to who should receive benefits.

The least amount of judgment occurs when an applicant has a disability which meets the listings since the task of the disability determiner is "merely" to decide whether an impairment coincides with any of the listings in the handbook. The regulations stress that the decision in this regard is to be made on the basis of medical considerations only. However, despite this emphasis, interviews with Disability Determination Service personnel suggested that administrative discretion sometimes occurs even at this stage in the disability-determining process, as when decisions regarding whether an applicant meets the listings are influenced by the reliability of the medical examination given to the applicant and by the background report prepared on the circumstances surrounding the impairment.

The regulations regarding the process of determining whether an applicant is entitled to benefits because a disability is "equal to" the listings also emphasize

---

*These provisions were the result of congressional reaction to the Kerner decision. See Chapter Three.

FIGURE 5.3

Percentage of Total Allowances and Denials, Excluding Technical Denials, San Francisco Region, 1970

Regulation	Definition	Decision	Percentage
1502(a)	(Denial only — medical considerations alone) Claimant not under a disability because his impairment is slight or minimal.	Deny	1.3
A1-1502(a)	(Medical considerations alone) Claimant's impairment meets the criteria in the listing of impairments.	Allow	22.7
B1-1502(a)	(Medical considerations alone) Claimant's impairment does not specifically meet the criteria in the listings but is equivalent in severity to those described there.	Allow	24.9
C1-1502(b)	(Medical plus vocational considerations) Allowance — individual has significant impairment plus adverse vocational factors.	Allow	10.5
	(Medical plus vocational considerations) Denial — individual has significant impairment but has the functional and vocational capacity to engage in substantial gainful activity.	Deny	31.7
D1-1502(c)	(Medical plus vocational consideration) (Allowance only) Older unskilled worker cannot do his usual arduous work because of a significant impairment.	Allow	00.4
1532	(Denial only) Individual is engaging in substantial gainful activity.	Deny	2.0
1501	Impairment severe but not expected to last 12 months or result in death.	Deny	6.3

Note: Percentages total less than 100.

Source: U.S., Department of Health Education, and Welfare, Social Security Administration, "Sequential Evaluation Process in the Adjudication of Disability Claims," *Regional SSA Program Circular,* D.F., no. 72-11-(49) S.F. 12/6/72.

that such decisions are to be based upon medical judgment exclusively. The signs, symptoms, and laboratory findings relating to the applicant's impairment or impairments must be found to be of equivalent severity to those of a specific section in the listings of impairments. However, disability-determining personnel suggest that this aspect of disability determination allows for an additional dimension of judgment because the results of the medical exam and the background report can only *suggest* the extent to which an impairment is equal to the listings.

A respondent in one state Disability Determination Service stated that this stage of the decision-making process is "largely judgmental," mainly because the meaning of the term "equivalent" is so subjective. This same response was elicited from members of a Western state Disability Determination Service who suggested that the "equal to" phrasing led to "considerable judgment" on the part of disability insurance examiners. Persons interviewed in a Southern Disability Determination Service remarked that the problem of determining whether or not a claimant can perform substantial gainful activity has become the focus of attention even in this stage of the decision-making process.

The uncertainties associated with claims involving disabilities that are equivalent to the listings is suggested by the following case provided by a state DDS as an example of the problems they encountered.*

> The applicant initially applied after breaking an arm and claiming that the impairment was a disability entitling him to benefits, since it kept him from engaging in substantial gainful activity. The claim was denied.
>
> The applicant then appealed under the provisions provided for reconsideration of initial denials, claiming that severe depression had resulted from the impairment. The claimed depression was confirmed by medical and psychiatric testimony. The depression presumably came from his inability to adjust to the disability. The claim was then allowed on the grounds that it was now equivalent to Listing 12.01 dealing with "mental" impairments.
>
> After a year the case was reviewed.† It was then determined that "significant" improvement had been made and although there was some depression, it was not severe. This was verified by the medical consultants within the state disability determining unit. As a result allowance payments were terminated.
>
> This decision was once again appealed under the provisions for reconsideration with the claimant contending that "significant" improvement had *not* been made. The decision was in favor of the claimant and the benefits were once more allowed.

---

*Interviews conducted in July 1974.
†Such cases are usually "diaried" for future review.

It is perhaps because of these problems that the provisions of regulation D1-1502(c) are so convenient. An older applicant with significant impairment may be granted benefits if he has a marginal education, and a long work experience in arduous, unskilled, physical labor which he is no longer able to perform.

This provision was adopted originally to provide benefits for "worn out" manual laborers, who "are not willing to go very far from their established homes, or to accept retraining for sedentary jobs, even though theoretically they might have sufficient residual functional capacity to perform some gainful employment" (Dixon 1973, p. 55). Such rationale obviously strays from the original legislative intent that applicants be denied benefits if they are able to engage in some form of substantial gainful activity.

But it is the borderline cases suggested by Regulation C1-1502(b) that permit the greatest discretion on the part of state disability determiners and are, therefore, the source of greatest controversy. Dixon claims that "the standards derivable from the law, the regulations, and Disability Insurance Letters [which are included in the DISM] are not worth a thing" because in such cases "the determinations must be non-medical to a significant degree" since they "are keyed to a mystical concept of theoretical residual employment capacity in simple jobs wholly unlike the claimant's past work and that exist in significant numbers in several regions if not locally" (Dixon 1973, pp. 57-58).

The Nagi survey, which studied the consistency of decisions regarding disability insurance, noted that determining whether benefits should be given to applicants with residual functional capacity under such circumstances amounted to little more than a toss of the coin (Nagi 1969b). This seems to be the case despite valiant efforts by the Social Security Administration and some state Disability Determination Services to prescribe precise administrative guidelines for determining who is eligible for benefits under C1-1502(b). This is reflected by the detailed specifications covering such cases in Figure 5.4.* Even with this specificity much discretion remains with the disability determiner about the importance of an applicant's age, residual functional capacity, skills, and education. For instance, the determiner still must decide whether the applicant can do his "usual work" and if not "what kinds of work he can do." Additionally, it must be determined "what employment opportunities" there are "for a man who can do only what the applicant can do" (U.S., Department of Health, Education, and Welfare, Social Security Administration 1972).

The importance of administrative judgment in such borderline cases was confirmed by the reactions of disability-determining personnel to the guidelines prescribed for allowance of claims under this regulation. For example, most administrators interviewed agreed that the 1967 amendments to the Social Security Act requiring that job availability be explored in an applicant's region of employment or "in several regions of the country" before awarding benefits

---

*Information gathered from interviews taken in July 1974.

FIGURE 5.4
Guidelines for C1-1502(b) Cases

Age	RVC[a]	Skills	Education	Decision
Any	Less than full range of sedentary	Any	Any	Allow
40 and above	Sedentary or narrow range of light	No special skills	Illiterate and language barrier	Allow
45 and above	Sedentary or narrow range of light	No special skills	Illiterate or language barrier	Allow
49 and below	Sedentary (and up)	No special skills	6 + (basic educational competencies)	Deny
50 and above (at least approaching advanced age)	Sedentary or narrow range of light	No special skills	Up to 12	Allow
	Sedentary	Transferable skills (must cite at least semi-skilled jobs	9-12	Deny
	Light	No special skills	Illiterate or language barrier	Allow
50-54	Upper extremity limitation	No special skills	Up to 12	Allow
	Light (and up)	No special skills	9-12	Deny
55-59	Light	No special skills	Up to 12	Allow
Advanced age	Light	Transferable skills (must cite at least semi-skilled jobs	9-12	Deny
	Medium	No special skills	6 +	Deny[b]
60 and far advanced age	Sedentary, light, or medium	No special skills	Up to 12	Allow
	Sedentary or light	Highly marketable skills transferable to closely related *skilled work*	8 +	Deny
	Medium	Transferable skills closely related to semi-skilled work	8 +	Deny

[a] Residual Functional Capacity
[b] Deny unless meets D1-1502(c) requirements
Source: Developed from Vocational Specialist Training (SSA) October 1972 (Oakland Office, California Disability Determination Service).

98

was being ignored because it was not realistic.* One state Disability Determination Service director noted that the national economy standard was of no consequence and that only opportunities for employment in the immediate area were relevant decisions regarding the available of substantial gainful activity. A regional representative for Disability Insurance supported this contention by noting that the "area of the state where the applicant resides" is the appropriate geographic area to consider in determining the availability of substantial gainful employment for a claimant.

There were exceptions to this lenient attitude, however, as in the case of the director of a state Disability Determination Service who interpreted the 1967 amendments literally and thus indicated that claimants should be denied benefits if substantial gainful activity for which they were suited were available in their region or in the national economy in general. In his view, this position was justified since any other policy would change the program from an insurance-oriented to a "social welfare" program. (The argument was reminiscent, interestingly, of the anti-collectivist's position as expressed during the course of debate over the adoption of disability insurance.) Interviews in a Southern state Disability Determination Service elicited a difference of opinion on this issue between two administrators. One insisted upon using the "national economy" standard and denying claims to those for whom jobs are available somewhere in the country, while the other argued that "concern about his state" should be taken into consideration when making a decision about whether benefits should be given.

In order to determine whether there is substantial gainful work available which the claimant can perform, the disability determiner relies upon the *Dictionary of Occupational Titles* (DOT), which lists the types of jobs theoretically present in a particular state or region. Some supplement this information with census data and information from the most recent *County Business Patterns.*

Opinions differ, however, on DOT's usefulness as a realistic indicator of the availability of substantial gainful employment in a particular region and on its proper place among the criteria for determining whether claimants should receive disability benefits. One disability determiner in a Northern state insisted that the DOT manual was followed very closely in determining whether positions were available which a claimant with a particular level of residual functional capacity could perform. He explained that if the manual listed such jobs the claim was denied on the ground that substantial gainful employment was available to the applicant. However, a supervisor of disability determiners within the same state DDS indicated that there is "extreme discretionary power" in the hands of disability determiners in allowing or denying benefits based on available substantial employment. He admitted encouraging the award of benefits in such borderline cases since it was really not feasible to expect a

---

*For further explanation of these amendments, see Chapter Three.

disability claimant to compete with a non-disabled person seeking a job. In his view, the job of the disability determiner is to serve the *claimant,* while still working within the framework of the rules and regulations prescribed by the Social Security Administration.

This same attitude is discerned in the responses of a number of other administrators interviewed. The director of one Disability Determination Service, for example, emphasized the importance of transferable skills in a "practical" sense, that is, the reasonableness of a person of a particular age, educational background, and so on, finding another job given the types of employment opportunities available. A regional representative noted the example of a claimant with a "significant impairment" who was 55 years of age, had six years of education, and was not able to transfer his skills. He stated that this type of claimant would receive benefits even though there might be "theoretical" jobs listed in the DOT which the claimant could perform.

LEGISLATIVE INTENT AND THE ADMINISTRATIVE GUIDELINES

What this review suggests is that the administrative guidelines have indeed followed legislative intent. Thus, the initial guidelines sought to implement original legislative policy that benefits should be given only for inability to engage in substantial gainful activity because of medically determinable impairment. The 100-percent review originally performed by the Social Security Administration of all initial Disability Determination Service decisions was designed to assure that this policy was followed.

However, as Congress and the courts expanded the universe of potentially qualified applicants, the administrative guidelines also expanded to cover the possibility that applicants whose impairments were not included in the medical listings might be entitled to benefits. This was the point of the sequential evaluation process. The trend toward softening Congress's original goal for the program in 1956 was exacerbated by changing the review procedure for decisions made by state Disability Determination Service personnel.*

However, it would be erroneous to conclude that the early emphasis that benefits be given only to those with an inability to work because of a severe impairment has been abandoned. As congressional reaction to the Kerner case suggests, it still constitutes the major theme for the disability insurance program. Thus, administrative guidelines enforce the policy that the ability to engage in substantial gainful activity is unrelated to whether a job is available or an applicant would be hired if he applied for a job. In actual practice, a job the individual could perform must not exist in the local economy or in several regions of the

---

*In 1972, the 100-percent review was changed to five-percent and later replaced by a post-adjudicative review. See Chapter Three.

country before a determiner can conclude that substantial gainful activity is impossible for an applicant whose impairment does not meet or equal the listings. The 1967 amendments and the consequent administrative guidelines continue to emphasize the original concern that disability insurance should not provide benefits on the basis of an applicant's unemployment or financial need.

What we have, then, are administrative guidelines which apparently attempt to reflect two contradictory views of disability and congressional goals for the program. The first is that applicants are entitled to benefits only if it is medically determined that an impairment is so severe that substantial gainful activity is impossible. The second is that there may be impairments which, when combined with vocational considerations and an applicant's age, education, and skills, result in an inability to engage in substantial gainful activity. To some extent this is an acknowledgement of the complex nature of disability and the fact that impairment is not the sole base and equivalent of disability.

PROFESSIONALISM AND DISABILITY DETERMINATION

The prevalence of highly professional personnel should have an influence upon how decisions are made regarding who receives disability benefits. Such personnel should be qualified for their jobs by virtue of their education, background, training, and experience; knowledgeable about the disability insurance program; intimate with the administrative guidelines; and dedicated to performing the task of disability determination as objectively and expeditiously as possible.*

In this section the importance of Disability Determination Service professionalism to decision making regarding award of benefits is assessed. Our major hypothesis is that states with a high degree of professionalism within their DDS will have lower award rates. Low award rates should occur in such states because of the propensity of professional personnel to abide by the underlying intent of the program, to approve benefits only if substantial gainful activity is impossible because of a medically determinable impairment.†

---

*Sharkansky lists similar attributes of professionalism when he indicates that highly professional administration results from personnel with advanced training in their fields of specialization, an active concern to stay abreast of the latest developments, and a desire to implement the most advanced level of service available (Sharkansky 1971, p. 261).

†Although the state Disability Determination Services render decisions on the federal program of disability insurance, are subject to guidelines from the Social Security Administration, and are totally funded by the federal government, they remain subject to state personnel practices and the exigencies of a state's economic and political situation. These factors have resulted in varying qualifications for disability-determining personnel and occasional refusal by state budgetary authorities to approve positions and the level of financial support authorized by federal funding (U.S. Congress, House, Committee on Ways and Means 1974, p. 19). This situation was also noted in interviews conducted with Disability Determination Service personnel, July 1974.

We have already noted the detailed administrative specifications which exist to establish objective standards for disability determination and that these standards were designed to limit disability benefits to only those who are clearly qualified. Given these guidelines, it is suggested here that Disability Determination Services with a high degree of professionalism will adhere closely to the criteria established by the Social Security Administration as specified in the sequential evaluation process and the memoranda included in the DISM. The fundamental result of such a policy should be reduced rates of awards because the guidelines establish the objective that disability benefits should be given because of the nature of an impairment rather than the condition of the state's labor market or the applicant's personal characteristics.

In order to assess the validity of this assumption, 12 criteria of administrative professionalism within state Disability Determination Services were chosen to measure this factor. These 12 criteria constitute four broad categories of administrative professionalism: agency expenditures, agency efficiency, agency judiciousness, and borderline allowance rates*.

Agency Expenditures: Percent of expenditures on medical exams, 1970; dollars spent per employee, 1970; nonmedical dollars spent per case, 1970; average salary for disability examiner, 1970.

Agency Efficiency: Percent of cases completed which were initial determinations, 1970;† average elapsed time for not developed cases, 1969-71; average elapsed time for developed cases.

Agency Judiciousness: Percent of initial allowances returned for substantive reasons, 1970; percent of initial denials returned for substantive reasons, 1970; percent of initial cases returned to state on which the state agency reverses its decision from allow to deny, 1970.

Borderline Allowance Rate: Percent allowed for listing A1, 1969 (medical listings); percent allowed for other than A1 or B1, 1969 (borderline and arduous cases).

Assumptions Regarding Levels of Professionalism within State Disability Determination Services

It was assumed that generous financial support would be considered essential to highly professional administrators.‡ For this reason, high levels of

---

*Borderline cases were defined for this purpose as those falling within C1-1502(b) and D1-1502(c), both of which require that decisions be made on the basis of medical plus "vocational factors." See Figure 5.2.

†Each state Disability Determination Service considers cases at the initial and reconsideration levels.

‡An opinion survey of 933 state administrators confirms that expansion of expenditures is considered an important ingredient of professionalism (Wright 1967).

expenditures for each of the characteristics constituting agency expenditures signify the dominance of professional expertise. Percent of expenditures on medical exams in 1970 refers to expenditures within Disability Determination Services for additional medical examinations to supplement available medical information about the claimant's impairment and ability to engage in substantial gainful activity. A professionally oriented agency should seek such information in order to have as much objective information as possible before making a decision. The number of dollars spent for each employee in 1970 suggests the level of overall support for the Disability Determination Service, whereas nonmedical dollars spent per case completed is a more specific indicator of financial support. A high average salary for disability examiners was considered an obvious commitment to obtaining professionally oriented personnel to engage in the disability-determining process.

The elements of agency efficiency, the second category of administrative professionalism, were chosen on the assumption that a highly professional Disability Determination Service would expedite the processing of disability claims. It was anticipated that this would be reflected by a high percent of cases completed in 1970 which were initial determinations, a low average elapsed processing time taken for not developed and developed cases. (A developed case is one for which additional medical information is necessary.)*

Regarding administrative judiciousness, it was assumed that a highly judicious state DDS would abide so closely to the standards prescribed by the Social Security Administration that the SSA would overturn a relatively low percentage of its decisions, indicated by a low percent of allowances and denials returned to the state agency by the SSA for further consideration.† (Until 1972 all initial determinations made by state Disability Determination Services were reviewed by the Social Security Administration.)

The agency borderline allowance rate category was designed to reflect the rate at which disability determiners grant allowances based on impairments that meet the medical listings (A1-1502a) as compared to the rate of allowances granted for impairments that do not meet or equal the listings. As noted, the medical listings most strongly reflect the objective that an applicant should be prevented from engaging in substantial gainful activity because of a medically

---

*The Social Security Administration has prescribed that processing time be seven days from receipt in the Disability Determination Service for not developed cases; 35 days from receipt in the DDS for developed cases that do not require a "consultative" examination; and 60 days from receipt for developed cases that do require such an examination. See U.S., Congress, House, Committee on Ways and Means 1974, tables 13, 22, pp. 159, 170-71.

†Data on these measures are for the year 1970 and are taken from *ibid.,* Tables 33, 38, pp. 209, 215. Technically the Social Security Administration may only "consult" with the state agencies about denials with which it disagrees since it is assumed that SSA should not be more lenient than the DDSs. In fact, however, both denials and allowances are returned to the states for their reconsideration.

determinable impairment before benefits are allowed. Other regulations associated with the sequential process reflect the need to accommodate applicants with impairments that do not meet or equal the listings. If the dominant theme of the disability insurance program is indeed a stress upon medical determinability, then a highly professional Disability Determination Service should reflect this situation by having a low rate of awards for borderline claims and a high rate of awards for impairments meeting the medical listings.*

Application Rates, Professionalism, and Disability Determination

Before analyzing the relationship between the measures of administrative professionalism and the rate of awards relative to the disability-insured population, let us briefly consider the impact of the press of work in the DDS on these administrative items. The data in Table 5.1 indicate that some of the components of administrative professionalism are subject to the effects of the rate, that is, the volume of applications for disability benefits. This is apparent in regard to the low percent of cases allowed that meet the medical listings (1038) when there is a high rate of applications. This possibly suggests that when various conditions result in a high rate of applications for disability benefits more of the applicants have marginal disabilities which, therefore, fall within borderline considerations. Indeed, the higher prevalence of borderline allowances (1040) with a high application rate suggests this possibility. Volume also seems to influence other administrative characteristics since a high rate of applications relates to a lower percentage of completed cases being initial determinations (1028), a higher percentage of expenditures for medical exams (1018), less nonmedical dollars spent per case completed (1022), less time taken for processing developed and not developed cases (1031 and 1032), and a lower percentage of returned cases on which the state reverses its decision from allow to deny. A low average salary for disability examiners, considered an indication of the absence of professionalism, is also associated with higher application rates. However, it is improbable that

---

*The data that specify allowances by state DDSs indicate that in 1969, 297,400 allowances were granted, with approximately 40 percent meeting the listings (A1-1502[a]); 40 percent equivalent to the listings (B1-1502[a]); and 20 percent in the borderline areas where decisions were based on medical and vocational factors. Approximately 18 percent of the allowances granted in the borderline cases were made under the most judgmental stage of the sequential evaluation process, C1-1502(b). It should be noted that this figure is higher than the estimate provided by Robert Dixon and specified in the *Regional Program Circular* for the San Francisco region and that it does not indicate the percent of denials under C1-1502(b). See earlier sections of this chapter.

The authors are grateful to Mr. Frederick Arner and Ms. Christi White for providing the data specifying the number of allowances for each stage of the sequential process. Mr. Arner and Ms. White were primarily responsible for the preparation of the *Committee Staff Report on the Disability Insurance Program*, 1974.

TABLE 5.1

Correlations between Application (Initial Allowance) Rates per
Disability-Insured Population and Twelve DDS Administrative
Professionalism Variables

Variable		Correlation with Application Rate
1018	Percent of expenditures on medical exams, 1970	.5101[a]
1019	Dollars spent per employee, 1970	.2392
1022	Nonmedical dollars spent per case completed, 1970	-.4508[a]
1028	Percent of cases completed which were initial determinations, 1970	-.4763[a]
1031	Average elapsed time for not developed cases, 1969-71	-.3911[a]
1032	Average elapsed time for developed cases, 1969-71	-.3733[a]
1033	Percent of initial allowances returned for substantive reasons, 1970	.1715
1034	Percent of initial denials returned for substantive reasons, 1970	-.0059
1038	Percent allowed for listing A1, 1969 (meets listing)	-.3957[a]
1040	Percent allowed for listings other than A1 or B1, 1969 (neither meets nor equals listing)	.5597[a]
1061	Percent of initial cases returned to state on which state agency reverses its decision from allow to deny, 1970	-.3060[b]
1079	Average salary, disability examiner, 1970	-.3994[a]

[a]Significant at .01 level.
[b]Significant at .05 level.

this situation is the result of the high rate of applications. It does not seem plausible that salaries would be reduced because of a heavier workload. While it might be assumed to reflect the overall socioeconomic condition of the state, both measures being affected by negative circumstances, average examiner salary showed insignificant correlations with the percent of non-disabled families earning less than $4,000 per year and the percent of males and females under 65 in the labor force.

The potential impact of rate of applications on overall DDS operation is apparent when examining the four categories of administrative professionalism and their relationship to application rates. A DDS considering a large volume of disability claims grants more allowances for borderline applications, relatively less for cases that meet the medical listings, and expedites the consideration of the applications. The situation is mixed relative to the expenditure of agency funds. There are fewer nonmedical dollars spent per case completed, but a higher percent of expenditures on medical exams with a high rate of applications. The quality of decision making, as reflected by SSA return of decisions, seems unrelated to the volume of applications. However, when allowance cases are returned to the state, there is a lower percent reversed when the application rate is high.

These findings seem to provide support for an interpretation that to some extent application rates affect administrative professionalism. It has already been indicated that the rate of applications affects the rate of award of disability benefits (see Chapter Four).

Findings: Level of Professionalism and Award Rates

Our present concern is to determine whether professionalism, with its stress upon objectivity in decision making, is related to lower award rates, in view of the effect of high application rates on awards. In order to determine this, a multiple regression analysis was performed, the results of which are presented in Table 5.2. This table specifies the professionalism variables utilized in the stepwise multiple regression analysis and identifies the respective categories of administrative professionalism in which they fall.

Analysis of the relationships between the elements of professionalism and award rates tends to confirm our assumption that the prevalence of professionalism influences award rates. Ten of the 12 ingredients of professionalism explain 73 percent of the award rate variance. While nonmedical dollars spent per case completed, 1970, (1022) was the single best explainer of variance in rates of award in the stepwise multiple regression, its F-test was not significant.

The explanation of variance itself does not provide us with sufficient information from which to judge the importance of professionalism. As suggested earlier, the expected significance of professionalism was that there would be lower award rates in states with higher levels of professionalism. In order to

TABLE 5.2

Award (Allowance) Rate per Disability-Insured Population and DDS Administrative Professionalism Variables

Variable		Beta	F-Test	Multiple R^2
1022 I	Nonmedical dollars spent per case completed, 1970	-.2058	1.14	.2129
1040 IV	Percent allowed for listings other than A1 or B1, 1969 (neither meets or equals listing)	.0583	.27	.3578
1032 II	Average elapsed time for developed cases, 1969-71	-.2269	2.79	.4212
1019 I	Dollars spent per employee, 1970	.1300	.51	.4984
1079 I	Average salary, disability examiner, 1970	-.3578	9.18[a]	.5762
1033 III	Percent of initial allowances returned for substantive reasons, 1970	.4150	10.80[a]	.6439
1034 III	Percent of initial denials returned for substantive reasons, 1970	-.3797	8.27[a]	.6907
1038 IV	Percent allowed for listing A1, 1969 (meets listing)	-.2189	4.50[b]	.7085
1028 II	Percent of cases completed which were initial determination, 1970	-.1731	2.37	.7203
1018 I	Percent of expenditures on medical exams, 1970	.1830	.68	.7310
1061 III	Percent of initial cases returned to state on which state reverses decision from allow to deny, 1970	.1159	1.04	.7382
1031 II	Average elapsed time for not developed cases, 1969-71	-.0853	.52	.7419

Note: Roman numerals indicate category of administrative professionalism as follows: I – agency expenditures; II – agency efficiency; III – agency judiciousness; and IV – borderline allowance rate.
[a]Significant at .01 level.
[b]Significant at .05 level.

assess the validity of this assumption, it is necessary to consider how the components of professionalism relate to award rates. In regard to the ten measures that explain 73 percent of award rate variance, low award rates should occur when state Disability Determination Services have a higher percent of expenditures on medical examinations for disability applicants (1018), spend more dollars per employee for agency operations (1019); spend more nonmedical dollars per case completed (1022); have a higher percent of cases completed which are initial determinations (1028); have a lower average elapsed time for developed cases, 1969-71 (1032); have a lower rate of allowances and denials returned by the Social Security Administration for substantive reasons (1033, 1034); allow a higher percent of cases to applicants who meet the medical listings (1038); allow a lower percent of cases for other than "meets" or "equals" listings (1040); and provide higher average salaries for disability examiners (1079).

The assumption about the import of professionalism upon award rates is basically confirmed by the findings. The results of the analysis (see Table 5.2) indicate that four of the professionalism measures showed individually significant F-tests in explaining the state-to-state variance in award rates. Award rates were higher when low levels of professionalism exist as suggested by lower average salaries for disability examiners (1079), a high rate of initial allowances returned by the Social Security Administration for substantive reasons (1033), and a low percentage of allowances to applicants who meet the medical listings (1038).

The remaining professionalism variable with a significant F-test, the percent of initial denials returned for substantive reasons (1034), was related negatively to awards, that is, in the opposite direction from what was anticipated. This may be a multi-colinearity effect or it may be the confounding influence of application rates. With a high rate of applications we would expect that a high percent of the applications received would be "inappropriate for approval," and, as a result, the percent of denials returned for substantive reasons would be low. At the same time, the rate of awards relative to the disability-insured population would be high.

If we attempt to use application rate to explain return of decisions, we would expect the opposite situation for the return of allowances. With a high rate of applications related to a high rate of allowances for other than "meets" or "equals" the listings, we would expect the percent of allowances returned for substantive reasons to be high. However, neither the percent of denials nor allowances returned for substantive reasons (1033 and 1034) was influenced significantly by application rate, as can be seen by the sizes of the zero order correlations shown in Table 5.1. It may be that these two measures of agency judiciousness are responsive on a more pragmatic basis to the effect of a high rate of awards on the review mechanism and are, therefore, less indicative of professionalism. We would then expect — as indeed was found — a high rate of awards to result in many allowances but few denials being questioned and, as a result, returned for substantive reasons. The interrelationships among application rates, award rates, and the return of DDS decisions as a possible reflection of professionalism or concern for volume of awards remain unclear and warrant additional inquiry.

In evaluating the findings, it becomes apparent that the measure of agency expenditures, that is, average salary for examiners (1079), and of borderline allowance rates, or rate of allowances for cases that meet the medical listings (1038), are key measures in predicting award rates in the direction hypothesized. Thus, awards are higher when there is a low level of professionalism as suggested by lower than average salaries for disability examiners and a low percentage of allowances for "meets the medical listings" (1038).

These results suggest that the degree of an agency's administrative professionalism acts as a damper on award rates but that administrative professionalism may not be an independent determinant of disability award rates. The implication is that the rate of applications for SSDI benefits, as affected by the state's socioeconomic situation, constitutes the basic environment within which professionalism operates. Additional investigation should be undertaken to clarify this relationship.

A major consequence of this situation is that a highly professional state DDS must attempt to exercise control over awards despite the fact that the major predictor of award rates is not professionalism. Given this fact, the issue relates to the ability of professionalism to modify or control award rates by utilizing the criteria established for determining who is entitled to disability benefits. In this regard it appears that professionalism does exercise some influence over award rates.

6
CONCLUSIONS AND IMPLICATIONS

The data and discussion presented in this volume provide the basis for some specific conclusions and assumptions about disability and the Social Security Disability Insurance program as it is presently conceived and administered.

First, as to disability in general, it seems evident that the tendency for segments of the population to define themselves as disabled is closely linked to the economic and social situation in which they live. Specifically, the socioeconomic condition of the state as it fails to provide opportunities for − or is not "congenial" to − employment and as it can be characterized as a depressed economy is associated with higher self-reports of work-related disability. States that show these characteristics also have high rates of persons who have never worked despite no disability. The high correlation between these two factors and the relation between disability rates and a set of socioeconomic characteristics reflect the nature of disability as a measure of the potential for labor force participation. This potential is composed of two elements: the individual's ability to work and the opportunity structure the labor market provides. Disability is the failure to match these two. What our data show is that the rate of self-defined disability is higher when socioeconomic conditions indicate a more restricted opportunity structure for employment and is lower when these conditions are more favorable. These data do not detract from the individualized nature and importance of an underlying impairment. They do, however, imply that whether or not a given impairment is disabling relates not only to the loss of functional capacity suffered by the individual and his or her own residual capacities but also to the other half of the match, the circumstances of the labor market and economy.

The significant issue is that the population at large shows the impact of this set of assumptions in its own tendency to report self-defined disability. The Social Security Disability Insurance program does not incorporate such local aggregate socioeconomic aspects of disability into its standards for award of benefits or its concept of substantial gainful activity. However, it is only logical to assume that the self-definition as disabled is the first step in the process of application for and award of SSDI benefits for persons who are disability-insured. It is then appropriate to look at the more direct programmatic issue, the relationship between socioeconomic characteristics and the rate of application for SSDI benefits in the state.

From our data, we can conclude a significant relationship exists between socioeconomic characteristics of the state and rates of application for benefits; the more depressed the economy and the labor market, the higher the application rate. Also, the higher the application rate, the higher the rate of awards as a percent of the disability-insured population.

THE MATCH BETWEEN PROBLEM AND POLICY

What conclusions can we draw from these findings? The policy underlying the SSDI program assumes that a disability at a level of substantial gainful activity follows from an impairment with a concern only for individual factors but not state labor force or need factors. From our data it seems evident that this assumption is unwarranted. The relationships in our data suggest the population served has a different impression of the problem of disability and a different basis for action than was used as the foundation for policy and program development. The program as conceived is supposed to be responsive to a condition of inability to engage in substantial gainful activity by reason of health, not an inability to find work in a depressed economy. That we can explain a substantial proportion (78 percent) of the variance in state-to-state application rates by measuring socioeconomic characteristics with the primary explanatory variables related in the direction hypothesized suggests that the applicants used existing impairments to substantiate the claims but were prompted to apply by socioeconomic considerations.

This situation suggests that the problem of disability was misdefined in formulating a policy to deal with it. The policy seems to have assumed disability was conceptually different in a very critical way from other work-limiting situations. That is, a disabled person was conceived of as unable to do a substantial amount of work because of the effect of an underlying health condition but independent of the job market. The disabled were defined as limited in their ability to work even if jobs were generally available. The policy was designed very carefully to avoid providing benefits to those who chose not to work or were unemployed because of the general condition of the economy or the job market. However, this conception does not seem to have matched the realities of the problem in terms of factors related to disability self-definition or population application for benefits. It is in this sense that we refer to the policy toward dealing with the economic needs of the disabled through Social Security as a mismatch or an "imperfect fit" to the underlying problem of disability.

THE MATCH BETWEEN POLICY AND PROGRAM

While a tendency to apply for benefits based on socioeconomic considerations might result in many inappropriate applications given the intent of the policy, this is, in and of itself, not inconsistent with the policy objectives. However, what would we anticipate the outcome to be if the policy conceptions are realistic and the resultant program's administrative procedures are consistent with the policy objectives? Since a substantial portion of the variance in application rates is explained by socioeconomic factors we would expect that the higher the application rate the more need-oriented applications and, therefore, the lower the percent of applications processed which are allowed. While this happened, the correlation was -.42, explaining only about 18 percent of the variance in percent of applications allowed. This is not an indication of strong program response to applications which are potentially inappropriate based on the policy conceptions. On the other hand, the application rate and the rate at which disability-insured persons were awarded benefits are highly positively correlated. The relationship is strong enough to account for 85 percent of the variance. The higher the rate of applications the higher the rate of awards as a percent of the disability-insured population.

Is this performance acceptable in view of the policy objectives? If it is assumed that a higher rate of applications brings in more applications that meet the standards for a finding of disability, then there is no indication of program abuse. However, on a conceptual level, should a higher rate of applications bring in more that meet the program standards, especially when need factors are shown to be a good predictor of a high level of applications? Our contention is that this should not be the case given the original policy intent.

The program standards relate to an inability to engage in substantial gainful activity, and this inability should not be affected significantly by state labor force and need factors. Of course, there may be a heightened awareness of the program in states with more depressed economies and "inhospitable" labor markets which brings in more disabled applicants. However, it is doubtful that this increased program awareness would explain our findings on the relationship between socioeconomic factors and application rates and through this intervening variable award rates.

The explanation for these findings logically would seem to lie within either, or some combination of, two considerations. First, the workings of the determination process used in the program may have permitted need and the condition of the state economy and labor market to become factors specifically taken into account in decision making beyond what the policy or the legislated program intended. In this situation, the disability determination process for SSDI benefits as administered within the state is seen as responsive to pressures from the socioeconomic condition within the state. There are no systematic data in the study relative to this question. While an association exists between economic conditions and award rates this could be the result of an independent process of decision making on applications motivated by these conditions rather than a specific reaction of disability determiners to a state's economic situation.

The second consideration is that the program standards for inability to engage in substantial gainful activity, which are highly oriented toward medical impairments, do not represent standards for such inability appropriate for the whole working-age population. This situation could result in many persons who technically can meet the standards because they have legitimate health impairments being routinely employed above substantial gainful activity yet available to apply for and be awarded benefits under certain negative socioeconomic conditions.

Thus, when there is difficulty in getting and holding a job in the state more people with legitimate health or injury characteristics may apply for benefits. Since these people can meet the impairment listings or their equivalents, they will be awarded benefits independent of any particular emphasis placed on social and economic factors. The point at issue is not whether these people meet the listings, but whether their basis for applying for benefits is their health as a factor affecting their ability to engage in substantial gainful activity or the economic situation which restricts the ability to gain or hold a position in substantial gainful activity. The population with one or more chronic diseases by far exceeds the number who report themselves as disabled. This body of people with some level of impairment constitutes a vast reservoir of individuals who could define themselves as disabled if they found themselves in a restricted job market which, therefore, promoted and reinforced self-definitions of disabled as a result of their impairments.

The disability insurance program has focused on listings of medical impairments which have been equated to a general standard of disability for the average worker on the average job. This seems to have created a structure where disability is viewed in terms of its underlying medical cause rather than as the original policy intended as a limitation of function which inhibits substantial gainful activity and which itself resulted from a medically definable impairment. If this is the case, then the program standards represent an impairment standard which only for some people and only under some circumstances may result in a disability but do not represent a universally applicable standard of inability to engage in substantial gainful activity. The result of the program's focus on medical impairment as the equivalent of disability is that it is subject to a great deal of pressure in the form of applications based on economic circumstances.

To briefly rephrase our impressions, the explanation for the finding of a linkage between socioeconomic characteristics and program award rates through the intervening variable of application rates may be based on need or other economic factors being taken into consideration directly in the determination process or the implications of equating impairment to disability as just discussed. Independent of whether one or the other explanation or a combination of both is the most suitable explanation, there is a strong indication that the program as designed and implemented does not carry out the original intent of the policy underlying the program. The program was not to give benefits based on need. An inability to work based on impaired health was supposed to mean a resultant limitation in work capacity, not just the impaired health itself. This inability to work was supposed to be based on the performance limitations of the individual, not a restricted availability of jobs. The design and implementation of the program makes the policy intent vulnerable to alteration in its actual application. It is in this sense that we refer to the SSDI program as a mismatch to the policy it was intended to carry out.

PROGRAM ADMINISTRATION AND ITS IMPACT

At this point we can introduce another aspect of concern, the relationship between the separate state-to-state administration of the decision-making process of disability determination and the rate of award of SSDI benefits.

Interviews with disability insurance personnel in some of the regional Social Security offices and in state Disability Determination Services left the impression that the process of disability benefit determination does indeed tend to ignore the specifications established by the Social Security Administration in favor of judgments by disability determiners that an applicant ought to receive benefits because of the unavailability of jobs or because of his or her general economic need. However, as pointed out, the results of these interviews must be used with care because of the limited number of respondents and because they do not provide data as to whether any association between need and awards exists because disability benefits were awarded as a reaction of determiners to a state's economic situation or on the basis of an independent decision-making process.

The concept of administrative professionalism was used in the analysis presented to discern the influence of state disability determining units upon award rates because of the contention that an agency with a high level of professionalism would tend to follow the objective agency guidelines in the process of making decisions. Under these circumstances it was hypothesized that highly professional Disability Determination Services would tend to follow the objective specifications prescribed by the Social Security Administration for determining who should receive benefits and consequently would permit disability benefits only if it were clear that the applicant was so disabled that substantial gainful activity was impossible.

The twelve variables used to measure administrative professionalism fell within four construct categories. These variables were analyzed for their influence upon award rates. It was hypothesized that a high level of professionalism should result in a low rate of disability awards. The twelve professionalism characteristics studied explained 74 percent of the variance in award rates. Of the four individual items with significant F-tests at the .05 level or better, three related in the direction hypothesized.

High levels of professionalism apparently are important as an administrative deterrent to high award rates. However, various of the administrative professionalism measures studied showed the influence of a high rate, that is, a large volume of applications processed within the DDS. Given this situation, it becomes obvious that professionalism has to be considered within the context of a high rate of applications, in turn affected by a state's socioeconomic characteristics.

Of importance was the fact that the findings regarding the impact of level of professionalism upon awards permitted an overall assessment of the influence of administrative professionalism. The qualifications of the disability examiners, as indicated by their salary levels, is the ingredient of agency expenditures of concern, since the prevalence of higher average salaries for examiners is related to lower award rates. A high rate of borderline allowances, as indicated by a low rate of award for "meets the listings," relates to higher award rates. Finally, agency efficiency is not an administrative characteristic that tends to control the level of disability awards but is primarily a function of the work load facing disability determining units.

In essence, then, levels of professionalism within an agency have some importance as a deterrent to the pressure to grant awards created by high application rates which may be related to a state's socioeconomic environment.

DIMENSION OF THE MISMATCH BETWEEN PROGRAM AND POLICY EXPECTATIONS

Program specifications for disability insurance under Social Security were in a number of ways a mismatch to the general policy they were intended to implement. While some of this is due to mistaken assumptions in the policy, the rest is due to difficulties in the specifications themselves. Of the many dimensions along which such incongruencies might have become manifest, we select five as particularly important: jurisdictional levels; rehabilitation; drawing clear distinctions between unemployment caused by disability and that caused by other factors; the use of impairment as an indicator of disability; and establishing a dichotomy between disabled and non-disabled.

Jurisdictional Levels

The structure of government in the United States raises important issues concerning the place and operations of public programs, including those related to disability. Of the multiple levels of government, the federal and state jurisdictions are most significant in this respect. Some programs are strictly federal in funding and administration, such as those of the Veterans' Administration. Others are state programs, such as Workers' Compensation and Temporary Disability Insurance. Still other programs represent a variety of arrangements between federal and state governments.

Public rehabilitation services constitute an example of agencies operating under state-federal arrangements. These programs are financed by both state and federal appropriations on the basis of formulae by which state funds are matched with those from federal sources according to a predetermined ratio. Although the ratio is lopsided, with a much higher federal contribution, the total funding for a state operation is actually controlled by the level of state appropriations. The role of the Rehabilitation Services Administration, the federal agency responsible for this program, is primarily to set up regulations for the use of federal funds, to develop standards and criteria for the provision of services, to evaluate innovative programs and projects for special grant support, and otherwise to coordinate the efforts of the state agencies. The direct administrative responsibility for program operations rests with the state agencies.

Disability Determination Services (DDS) in the various states, which evaluate and adjudicate applications for disability insurance benefits under Social Security, represent another type of arrangement involving state and federal levels of government. Although the Social Security programs fall within federal jurisdiction, the amendments authorizing disability insurance specify that the function of evaluation and adjudication be performed by appropriate agencies of the states.

Agreements between the Social Security Administration and the states resulted in the creation of the DDSs, which are fully financed by federal funds but administered by state agencies. In most of the states, disability determinations are administered by rehabilitation agencies and by welfare agencies in a few others. In addition to specifying regulations and setting up criteria and standards, the Social Security Administration, as previously mentioned, conducts reviews of a sample of adjudications made at the state level.* The SSA can reverse a state determination to allow benefits, but it does not have the authority to reverse a state denial. In practice, however, state denials considered questionable by reviews in the national office are returned for further assessment, and a resolution of differences is usually reached.

---

*Originally this was done on a 100-percent basis. In 1972 it was changed to a five-percent sample review. Additionally, the review was later changed from pre-adjudicative to post-adjudicative.

Unlike comparable units of government administering totally federal or totally state programs, agencies combining state-federal involvement occupy a position that usually affords them greater independence. Their administrative relationships, where the lines of authority and sanctions reside, are with state governments where usually technical knowledge for evaluating the performance of such agencies is underdeveloped. On the other hand, the corresponding federal agencies, which have specialized knowledge and evaluative capabilities concerning the respective programs, do not have direct administrative influence on the state agencies. The primary leverages available to agencies at the federal level are withholding funds and auditing the operations of state agencies. The first leverage is too extreme for realistic application, and the second is often rendered ineffective by the nature of agency activities, especially in service programs, and the types of records generated. Most auditing procedures have been fiscally rather than program-oriented. There are other leverages, but their collective influence would seem to be less than that of a direct relationship combining both technical knowledge and administrative authority. The administrators and personnel of organizations such as the ones described above soon become adept in using the dual administrative and technical relationships to state and federal authorities for gaining greater independence in shaping their programs. In spite of federal regulations, such independence often leads to variation in operations which in turn undermines the highly sought standardized and uniform decisions on benefits and services.

Rehabilitation

One of the primary objectives in contracting disability determinations for benefits under social security to be carried out by agencies of vocational rehabilitation is to coordinate closely decisions about disability with those concerning rehabilitation services. The idea was that the rehabilitation potential of applicants would become a factor in benefits decisions and that those who could benefit from rehabilitation services would receive them. The structure that evolved, however, left the two operations (disability determination and rehabilitation) merely housed within the same agency but highly independent of each other. Furthermore, the gatekeeping criteria for the two purposes seem incongruous. Some cases allowed disability benefits under Social Security were screened out from rehabilitation with the reason given being that their disabilities are not sufficiently severe (Nagi 1969b). The reverse incongruency also occurs, that is, cases denied benefits presumably because the disabilities are not sufficiently severe are also denied rehabilitation services because the disabilities are too severe to be rehabilitated (Nagi n.d.). The lack of coordination between these two decisions can be very confusing to applicants and clients.

In 1965, amendments to the Social Security Act allowed the use of the Trust Funds for the rehabilitation of disabled beneficiaries. According to these statutes, a specified percentage of the cost of benefits is allocated for use by the state-federal programs of vocational rehabilitation to serve these beneficiaries. The intent was to increase the involvement of rehabilitation with the recipients of disability insurance benefits and to allow for the greater costs that such severely disabled persons would require. Because of the open-ended allocations to rehabilitation agencies without measures of accountability and the absence of checks and balances between the SSA and Rehabilitation Services Administration in managing this aspect of the program, the results have been disappointing. A study by the General Accounting Office of the rehabilitation of the "Trust Fund" cases shows that the effectiveness of these efforts falls far short of expectations (GAO 1976). In regard to the rehabilitation of disabled beneficiaries under Social Security, therefore, it can be said that while the general approach is well intended and meaningful, program specifications failed to meet the objectives. Rehabilitation services cannot be blamed fully for the difficulty, which stems in part from the many disincentives inherent in the current structure of benefits.

DISABILITY AND UNEMPLOYMENT

Another problem arises from attempts to make an absolute distinction between unemployment because of health reasons and unemployment because of labor market conditions or other non-health-related reasons. As has already been mentioned, in real life these sets of factors at times interact in precipitating or preventing disabilities. While program decisions tell us that a proportion of people apply for benefits without meeting the determination criteria, and thus their claims are denied, no data are available about the people who continue to work past the point when their health conditions would qualify them for disability benefits. Motivation, reaching certain points in the life or family cycle, employers' attitudes, and a whole host of other factors, most important of which is change in the labor market, can compel these people to seek disability benefits. To which factors should their disabilities be attributed? Should they be attributed to the health problems which these people endured until a critical incident occurred or a tighter market pushed them out of the labor force? Or are we to consider such incidents and change in the market as the causes for unemployment and deny them benefits? In short, expectations of the general policy to separate employment factors from health factors in a clear and consistent manner are, to say the least, unrealistic, and attempts to operationalize these expectations in program specifications have led to problems in equity and management. The increase in rates of applications and rates of allowances in relation to the population covered, at times of economic recession, should be anticipated rather than become a surprise and a cause for crisis management.

Insistence on separating employment factors from those of health in cases when interaction between the two is inevitable poses an important obstacle to the motivation of beneficiaries to return to work. The regulations specify that a beneficiary who leaves that status after a successful trial work period cannot requalify without a demonstrated change in the health condition that makes it more limiting. In other words, persons who qualify because of given health problems and who struggle to find work without change in their health conditions cannot requalify unless their health worsens. In fact, if their conditions have indeed worsened and they requalify, they must sustain another waiting period to regain Medicare coverage. Such rules can only help lock beneficiaries into that status once they qualify and therefore act as a disincentive to cooperation with rehabilitation efforts.

Impairment as an Indicator of Disability

An important distinction that needs to be made here is between concepts of attributes and relational concepts (Cohen 1957). The first type of concepts refers to properties and attributes of the objects being described, such as weight, height, and intelligence. Indicators for these concepts can all be found within individuals' characteristics. By contrast, the indicators of a relational concept cannot all be accounted for within individual units of analysis. Instead, some indicators are to be found in related segments of the situation.

To illustrate, we apply these distinctions to the concepts of impairment and disability. Physical impairment is a concept of properties and attributes; all of its indicators can be found in the individual. We need not go beyond examining the individual to identify the presence and extent of physiological and anatomical losses or disorders. On the other hand, the concept of disability is relational. Its indicators are found not only in the person pronounced disabled but in such other entities as the requirements of roles to be performed, the attitudes of others, and other situational factors. For example, although some of the indicators of vocational abilities/inabilities are intrinsic to the disabled, such as physical and mental capacities and limitations, vocational skills possessed, and motivation toward work; other indicators are of a situational nature, such as the physical and mental requirements of the work, the vocational skills required by the work, and the environmental factors that make employment accessible or inaccessible. To account for the various types and degrees of vocational inability, indicators for these various dimensions must be included. The interaction among all of these and related variables determines the presence and severity of disability.

Distinctions between concepts of attributes and those of relations were not observed in operationalizing the concept of disability for program purposes. Although changing over the years to account for the influence of other factors, a heavy if not an exclusive reliance was placed upon impairments as indicators of disability. That this has been the case in most insurance and compensation programs has led the AMA's Committee on Medical Rating of Physical Impairment to conclude that "impairment is, in fact, the sole or real criterion of permanent disability far more often than is readily acknowledged" (Committee 1960). Several reasons contribute to this reliance on impairments as criteria for disability. First is the interpretation of the term "cause" in the various statutes. Non-engagement in gainful activity may indicate disability, unemployment, or mere idleness. In order to draw the boundaries, statutes state that for non-engagement in gainful activity to be considered as an indication of disability it must have occurred *because* of the presence of impairments; the SSDI program legislation states there must be an inability to engage in substantial gainful activity because of an impairment. Often the term "because" is interpreted to mean that impairment is a necessary and sufficient cause for disability and that in this sense the two are equivalent. Differences between impairment and disability in definitions and indicators negate such interpretation, except in cases where impairments are so extremely limiting as to become the sole determinants of disability. However, in most cases, including those allowed benefits, impairments are only contributing factors. To interpret the term "because" as meaning necessary and contributing, rather than sufficient, cause would be more consistent with the nature of disability and would lead to more equitable decisions.

Another reason for emphasis on impairment is the attempt to differentiate sharply between disability benefits and those related to unemployment stemming from other factors. In some cases, the two phenomena are difficult to separate, especially at times of high unemployment. In a tight labor market, many persons with limitations in capacity may tend to seek disability benefits, especially when other characteristics such as age, education, and skills mitigate against retraining and reemployment. However, there seems to be a lack of recognition in program definitions of the simple fact that change in labor market conditions interact with limitations in capacity to produce work disabilities.

Even when multiple causal models of disability are accepted, agencies tend to operationalize the definitions around the more readily identifiable indicators and measurable criteria. In other words, because operational definitions emphasize the more measurable dimensions, they may depart from the original concepts. For example, "Impairments can be measured with a reasonable degree of accuracy and uniformity on the basis of loss of structural integrity, pathological findings, or pain substantiated by clinical examination" (Committee 1960). Equally significant but less easily measured factors, such as the influence of age, lack of skills, potential for retraining and placement, education, stigmatization, or disfigurement tend to get ignored. A report by the Subcommittee on the Administration of the Social Security Laws of the House Committee on Ways and Means issued in the late 1950s stated,

> The Subcommittee recognizes the difficulty of developing and enunciating specific criteria for the weight to be given nonmedical factors

in the evaluation of disability and the extreme sensitivity of this area. . . . But, the Subcommittee believed then that the time has come, if it is not well overdue, to make a determined effort to develop and refine these criteria and make them available to the evaluators and to the public in the form of published regulations." (Subcommittee on Social Security 1959).

This amounts to a mandate to look for the key where it was dropped rather than where the light happens to be.

Finally, the influence of the medical profession must be mentioned as a factor in the heavy reliance on impairment in the identification and measurement of disability. The visible level of involvement of organized medicine in congressional hearings concerning disability legislation attests to their interest in these matters. Aside from expressing general political and economic views about disability benefits, the medical profession's primary concern was with the role of physicians in such programs and the potential impact of government via these programs on the practice of medicine. With no counter-influence as strong as that of the medical profession, the statutes and regulations governing disability benefits were greatly tilted toward medical criteria. Thus, impairment and pathology, which in the main constitute medical knowledge, became the primary indicators and measures of disability. Knowledge about pathology and impairment can be used for a variety of purposes: preventive health practices, diagnosis, treatment, restorative care, or the evaluation of work disability. While physicians are well trained in the use of medical knowledge for purposes related to the identification and control of diseases and injuries, they seldom receive formal training in the use of this knowledge in assessing limitations in work.

The end result of this emphasis upon impairment is that the operational definitions and criteria for determining disability for insurance under Social Security are organized chiefly around listings of certain signs and symptoms. These are used as standards and, when found to exist, the applicant would be considered unable to engage in gainful activity. Combinations of unlisted symptoms and signs also would qualify a person for benefits when the severity equals those in the listings. The assumption, of course, is that signs and symptoms in the listings or their equivalences would draw the line between those who have the capacity to engage in substantial gainful activity and those who do not.

Dichotomizing a Continuum

Both policy and program specifications are based upon a dichotomy of disabled/non-disabled. Thus, decisions on disability benefits under Social Security are basically either to allow or to deny claims. Considering that disability represents a continuum, any point at which the line for a dichotomy is drawn will leave doubtful cases on both sides. Neither does the policy recognize this fact nor do the regulatory specifications provide special criteria or procedures to handle such cases. The only features that might have been addressed, at least in part, to ambiguous cases are reconsiderations, hearings, and appeals. However, reconsiderations are adjudicated on the basis of the same criteria, and hearings and appeals generally are pursued by the tenacious rather than by persons with ambiguous cases. Furthermore, the appearance of lawyers and/or physicians on behalf of claimants seems to be more significant to the outcome of hearings and appeals than the nature of the case (Rock 1969).

It might be argued that dividing a continuum into categories would always produce ambiguous cases around the cutting points. This is undoubtedly true; however, there is a basic difference in results between dichotomous and three or more categories. While ambiguous cases in a dichotomous system would be either denied or allowed, similar cases in a system of multiple categories would be accorded different levels of severity.

Another criterion used in defining disability for the purposes of Social Security insurance reinforces the dichotomous view of determinations, that is, the level of earnings considered as designating "substantial gainful activity." For persons to be eligible for benefits, their earnings must be below that level. The same criterion applies in regard to the termination of benefits in the sense that beneficiaries who successfully maintain earnings in excess of the SGA level throughout the trial work period are removed from the rolls. In addition to the arbitrariness of the levels at which SGA is set, the dichotomy they create and the low levels at which they are established add strong disincentives to beneficiaries' attempts to return to work. For example, in 1977, while the SGA was set at $230, the potential level of maximum family benefit reached a high of several times that amount per month. It does not require a highly rational economic mind to wonder about the advisability of losing benefits for such a low level of earnings.

Comparison with Other Disability Systems

While the policy and program specifications for disability insurance under Social Security vary in some respects from other programs, they entail many features common to some. For example, it can be said that this program is similar in both general policy and specifics to all of the disability insurance programs that are part of retirement and survivors benefits, such as those of public employees, railroad, and maritime workers. Disability insurance under these programs is heavily impairment-oriented in criteria, utilizes standard listings, and is organized around dichotomous decisions. However, none of them are faced with jurisdictional problems since they fall exclusively within one level of government or another. Rehabilitation efforts related to these latter programs are minimal and depend almost entirely on state-federal programs.

In contrast to disability insurance under Social Security, temporary disability insurance programs are oriented to short-term sickness. They are addressed to the effects of incapacitating pathologies and impairments. There is a heavy reliance on the judgment of physicians, who provide a diagnosis and an estimate of the length of time a claimant needs to remain away from work for recovery and convalescence. These data are part of the medical practices and physicians are trained to provide them with competence. In addition, the agencies administering temporary disability insurance programs have developed norms based on experience as to the length of time required for the various types of disorders (Spreitzer, Larson, and Nagi 1973). Significant deviations from these norms in the evaluations of given physicians prompt the agencies to seek additional opinions. There is little connection between temporary disability insurance and rehabilitation agencies, nor are these insurance programs faced with the problem of jurisdiction since they are state-operated.

Another important comparison is of Social Security disability insurance, on the one hand, and compensation programs, on the other. Two major programs of compensation are of special significance in this respect: veterans' benefits and workers' compensation. The two are addressed to a combination of objectives, especially indemnification for impairments sustained in the course of military service or connection with work and compensation for earning losses sustained because of service-connected or work-connected impairment, respectively. While these two programs share with disability insurance the heavy reliance on impairment as an indicator of disability, they recognized the continuum of disability and based their benefits on percentages of deviation from the "whole person." Thus, elaborate impairment schedules were developed in which the loss of a finger, for example, is rated at a certain percent and so is the loss of a hand, an arm, or a certain restriction in motion. The ratings are fairly arbitrary and bear little if any relation to actual loss in earnings. The veterans' programs are fully federal in finance and administration, and workers' compensation are either federal or state, with most of the programs falling within the jurisdiction of the states. There are great variations among the states in patterns of finance, modes of administration, coverage, and levels of benefits in relation to workers' compensation (*Report of the National Commission on State Workmen's Compensation Laws* 1962). If the rates of litigations are in any way indicative of the feeling of inequity stemming from either the policy or program specification workers' compensation programs can be considered among the least equitable.

Finally, a comparative assessment must include a statement about public assistance for the disabled who have no chance to establish eligibility in insurance and compensation programs. Administered earlier by welfare agencies, eligibility requirements for such assistance were based primarily upon need and secondarily upon health conditions. Although the element of need has retained some influence, since the programs were moved to the Social Security Administration a few years ago an attempt has been made to shift priority by emphasizing disablement as the primary consideration. Public assistance to the blind and the disabled, now part of Social Security's Supplemental Security Income (SSI) program, follows a similar pattern in criteria and administration as disability insurance except for the role of SGA in determining eligibility. Therefore, all issues outlined earlier in relation to disability insurance largely apply also to SSI.

SOME POSSIBLE "WHYS" FOR THE MISMATCH

The thrust of this presentation has been on the "match" and "mismatch" among the definitions of the problem .of disability for insurance purposes under Social Security, the general policy as reflected explicitly in the statutes and implicitly in legislative intents, and program specifications as incorporated in the formal regulations and procedures as well as in the informal aspects of the day-to-day operations. We need to explore the reasons for mismatches and possible recourses. However, before turning to these topics, we will first identify, by way of recapitulation, some of the important incongruencies.

To begin with, a problem such as disability can be defined in a variety of ways and from each would flow different approaches and specifications. For example, if disability were to be defined as an individual problem, little concern would be attached to it from the viewpoint of public policy. On the other hand, once defined as a social problem, disability became a legitimate object of public policy and programs. An important influence upon *when* a problem is defined as social is the predominate values in a society. Furthermore, while a definition may account for a problem's multidimensionality, the definition may be operationalized on the narrow basis of specific indicators and measures. This has been the case in definitions of disability under Social Security. While a meaningful definition would include a person's work capacities and limitations, work requirements, and chances for employment in view of prevailing attitudes and barriers, a narrow definition would be, and has been, limited to indicators of pathology and impairment. Finally, as noted earlier, social welfare problems in the United States tend to be defined from the perspective of the anti-collectivists or the reluctant collectivists. Reluctant collectivists (welfare-state liberals) tend to define disability insurance as a protection and assistance for the disabled. Anti-collectivists (traditional economic liberals — present-day conservatives) usually define disability insurance as a protection for the well-to-do against the dependency of others at times of misfortune. A more accurate assessment certainly would include both purposes. Although far from reaching a national consensus, the prevailing definitions of disability convey its designation as a social problem, operationalize it in the narrow terms of pathological indicators largely ignoring vocational and other factors, and consider disability insurance primarily as providing aid and protection to the disabled.

Difficulties with the policy stem partly from the definition of the problem. The attribution of disability to "medically determinable impairment" in the statutes without equal emphasis on other factors has greatly influenced the program toward a heavily medical rather than vocational or balanced orientation. As pointed out earlier, the assumption in the general policy that health conditions can be separated clearly from vocational factors in disability is inconsistent with the nature of the problem. Furthermore, the dichotomous view of presence or absence of disability grossly oversimplifies the multidimensional continua involved. On the other hand, the general policy entailed wisdom in recognizing the eventual need for further development in eligibility criteria to include the nonmedical factors and the advisability of a close link between disability insurance programs and rehabilitation services.

Program specifications are the collecting points for limitations in definitions and in perspectives shaping policy. In addition, these specifications added a few problems of their own. The overriding concern has been with the development of listings of pathologies and impairments without equal attention to other indicators and measures of disability.

The staffing patterns in the DDSs favor a strong role for medicine compared to vocational specialists and others with competence in nonmedical aspects of disability. While examiners are trained into working with and utilizing the consultation of physicians, they receive little if any formal training on the use of specialists from vocational and other fields. All of this adds up to the repeatedly mentioned overconcern with the health components compared to vocational and other factors in disability. The dichotomous decisions engender borderline and ambiguous cases with no specific rules for decisions when in doubt, and a substantial risk of denial (Nagi 1969b). In addition, this dichotomy along with the levels of earnings considered as indications of "substantial gainful activity" tend to lock clients into the status of beneficiary. Finally, the involvement of state governments in disability determinations has introduced variations in operations and decisions defeating the standardization required in the distribution of federally administered insurance benefits. Also, the close articulation of relations between disability insurance and rehabilitation services, intended by the involvement of state agencies, can hardly be declared effective.

Several factors account for these incongruencies and mismatches in problem definitions, policy, and program specifications. Among the more important are the level of knowledge and technology related to disability, the prevailing values and ideologies, the protection of political and professional domains, the nature of political processes in the United States, more concern with reliability than validity in determinations, and deference to routinization and administrative ease in decisions. These factors overlap and interrelate in a variety of ways.

Knowledge and Technology

Knowledge about the nature of disability, approaches to its classification and measurement, and explanations for its occurrence are fundamental to the formulation of clear, practical statues; and technologies determine the means available for meeting program objectives. Systematic analyses of concepts and differentiations of disability from related conditions started to enter the literature only in the early 1960s (Nagi 1965; Haber 1967). Meaningful data on disability and limitations in function were to follow during the latter part of the decade (Nagi 1969b; Haber 1968; Allan 1976; Nagi 1976). Measures of work capacities and limitations are underdeveloped, and measures of the types and levels of mental, emotional, and physical requirements of different jobs are virtually nonexistent. In summary, while verbal hypotheses abound, there is no quantitative theory of disability that meets the scientific tests of reliability and validity. Such knowledge is necessary for the identification of criteria and the weights they should be accorded in disability determinations, whether for benefits or for services.

In the absence of specific information about identification, measurement, causes, and distributions of a given social problem, political decisions tend to follow the power of persuasion and political influence. There is no basis for deliberations grounded in facts. The operationalization of program decisions would tend to lean more heavily toward aspects about which systematic knowledge and technology exist and hence the heavy reliance on medical information about pathology and impairment. It is important to note in this respect that compared to other national programs, such as health care, science, agriculture, and defense, disability receives very limited appropriations for research support. Furthermore, the overwhelming proportion of this support is spent in studying and developing intervention and restorative measures and counseling the disabled. Little attention is directed toward the development of approaches to identification, measurement, and explanation of the problem. Even research on intervention suffers greatly from the lack of basic understanding of the nature of the problem and the factors that precipitate it (Berkowitz et al. 1975).

Values, Interests, and Political Processes

Values play an important role in the definitions of problems and in shaping attitudes about government intervention and general policies when such intervention is acceptable and supportable. On the conception of social problems and the role of government in these respects, American values and attitudes are fairly divided. The most significant contrast in regard to disability insurance and benefits is between what we have called the anti-collectivists and the reluctant collectivists.* To the first group, most problems are the result of individual defects and an inability or unwillingness to cope. If they wish, people can pull

---

*See Chapter One. The anti-collectivists have also been described as individualists, economic liberals, and laissez-faire evolutionists, while the reluctant collectivists have been described as collectivists, welfare state liberals, and equalitarians.

themselves up by their bootstraps; market mechanisms and private resources should meet their needs. Government intervention to assist is viewed as interference with the natural course of evolution and the natural laws of the market to the detriment of both. In the eye of holders to these values, to institute public programs for disability benefits would be tantamount to encouraging idleness, malingering, and cheating.

Reluctant collectivists, on the other hand, attribute social problems more to structural than individual factors. Thus, it is the structure of the labor market and technology that exposes certain categories of people to greater risks of disabling disease and injury. It is the nature of the economic structure that deprives given classes of people of a healthy environment, access to health care, and the opportunity to accumulate resources sufficient to maintain economic independence in times of disability or other interruptions in earnings. To this group, equality and freedom are attainable only when the burden of need for basic necessities is lifted. They see a major role for government and public programs in alleviating such needs. Varying gradations of values fall between these two contrasting positions. Leaning heavily in the direction of medical criteria was undoubtedly an attempt to pacify adherents to the first set of values by assuring the use of objective medical knowledge and technology to rule out benefits for the undeserving idler or malingerer. The lay public is in a position neither to evaluate the objectivity of medical knowledge about pathology and impairment nor to evaluate its relevance to disability determinations.

Disability insurance programs touch the interests of many groups. Among the most concerned are labor unions, whose interests lie in the welfare of workers and social economic security. Organized labor has always been a supporter of new legislative initiatives in relation to income maintenance in times of sickness, disability, and unemployment. They also have constituted an important influence in liberalizing existing programs over time. On the other hand, business groups usually are concerned with the costs of such programs and their influence on the prices they have to charge for their products. A sector of the business community with particular interest in disability benefit programs under Social Security is that of insurance, where public programs are considered a threat to private enterprise.

The protection of professional and organizational domains constitutes another aspect of the influence of interest groups on political processes and outcomes. Warren's conception of organizational domain, applicable also to professions, is helpful analytically:

> Organizational domain is the organization's locus in the interorganizational network, including its legitimized "right" to operate in specific geographic and functional areas and its channels of access to task and maintenance resources. The two important components here are the organization's right to do something, and its access to the resources it needs in order to do it. (Warren 1972)

As pointed out earlier, organized medicine considered legislation on disability insurance as of significant interest to the medical profession, and so did vocational rehabilitation counselors and others involved in the helping professions. Once programs are introduced, new agencies are created to administer them and new professions or specialties may arise to man them. There was no exception in this respect in regard to disability insurance where a federal unit was created within the Social Security Administration, disability determination agencies were developed in the various states, and the new profession of disability examiner has emerged and is maturing into specialized curricula leading to the Masters degree. These organizations and professions have vital interests in statutory and operational change in programs. They are most likely to support expansion of domains and the preservation of familiar approaches and procedures.

As discussed earlier, another feature of policy making in the United States that accounts for some of the limitations in approaches is incrementalism. Paraphrasing Charles E. Lindblom, Dye describes the process as follows:

> Decision makers do *not* annually review the whole range of existing and proposed policies, identify societal goals, research the benefits and costs of alternative policies in achieving these goals, rank-order preferences for each policy alternative in terms of the ratio of benefits to costs, and then make a selection on the basis of all relevant information. On the contrary, constraints of time, intelligence, and cost prevent policy makers from identifying the full range of policy alternatives and their consequences. Constraints of politics prevent the establishment of clear cut societal goals and the accurate calculation of cost-benefit ratios. The incremental model recognizes the impractical nature of "rational-comprehensive" policy making, and describes a more conservative process of decision making. (Dye 1972, p. 30)

Incrementalism implies an evolutionary process toward greater rationality in statutes and regulations. However, it should be noted that groups and organizations whose domains are involved often exert influence toward optimizing or maximizing their interests rather than toward rational change. This is perhaps one of the most important reasons organizations resist research on their structural and operational problems.

The Routinization of Decisions and the Issues of Reliability and Validity

Public programs tend toward the routinization of decisions through reliance on simple and objective criteria (Nagi 1974). Thus, age becomes a criterion for admission to public schools and for receiving retirement benefits. Often these criteria represent complex phenomena, such as age in relation to the level of maturity that qualifies a child for certain levels of instruction. To attempt to organize a decision-making structure around the actual measurement of maturity would be administratively cumbersome and financially prohibitive. Furthermore, because of the lack of precise quantitative knowledge about the phenomenon, decisions based on a complex evaluation would invite a litigious atmosphere. No one simple objective indicator can represent disability in the way age has been used for school admission or retirement. However, impairment and pathology served the purpose of objectivity, if not simplicity.

Specific and objective criteria do not lead only to routinization of decisions but also to enhancing their reliability. By reliability we mean reaching the same results when decisions over the same case are repeated. Reliability does not indicate that such decisions are necessarily valid; that is, decisions can be consistent but in error. However, in the quest for routinization, emphasis on reliability gives a sense of administrative justice which is attained when objective criteria are applied to all cases, even when they do not accurately identify and measure the phenomenon under consideration.

If routinized and nonroutinized decision models represent two ends of a continuum, disability determinations fall somewhere in the middle. They are not totally lacking in objective criteria and therefore based on pure subjective assessment; nor are all relevant criteria known, quantified, and weighted. Pressure toward routinization has led to the development of the standard listings of pathology and impairment. The use of these listings assures some degree of reliability and uniformity, facilitates the organization of decision making, and also conveys a sense of justice. However, they remain open to questions of validity and equity.

Recourse and Implications for Policy

There are certain policy implications attached to the totality of findings from the various aspects of this analysis which suggest possible alternatives for the SSDI program. It seems evident that the disability insurance program is not accomplishing its original objectives. That is, it is not providing an insurance protection for the covered population against the unique risks of an inability to engage in substantial gainful activity because of health reasons. The data on state socioeconomic factors related to application rates and on the relationship between application and award rates indicate that the program is far more reflective of and responsive to aggregate need and labor force characteristics than was intended. The acceptability of this situation is a value judgment and not amenable to data analysis. However, certain policy alternatives and their implications can be reviewed briefly.

Disability insurance under Social Security does not exist or operate in a vacuum; there are several other federal, state, and private programs addressed to benefits, compensation, and assistance for the disabled. To insure increasing compatibility and consistency, comprehensive reforms involving changes in these programs are advisable. The aim should be toward better articulation among the roles of the various programs as well as between them and rehabilitation services. In these concluding remarks, however, we will confine the discussion to points specific to Social Security Disability Insurance. Three areas need to be given priority in consideration for change and development: criteria of determination, barriers to movement from and return to the status of a beneficiary, and the jurisdictional question concerning decisions and reviews.

Criteria of Determination

It would be possible to establish new standards for disability using either of two approaches. If the primary concern is to reduce the disability rolls and the cost of the program while maintaining the current heavy emphasis on impairment standards, a stricter definition of disability in terms of medical impairments could be established. Under such a system, an applicant not working at a level of substantial gainful activity would have to meet the exacting standards of a detailed listing of impairments or an equivalent impairment as determined under far more rigid rules than presently exist. Applicants whose disabilities did not meet these standards would receive public income maintenance payments only under a program oriented to need determination or unemployment compensation.

However, the choice is not between criteria that structure decision making around pathology and impairment, on the one hand, and a nonstructured, totally individualized determination because of absence of criteria, on the other. A conceptually and empirically rooted change more in keeping with the nature of disability and the original policy intent would take two directions. First, is to develop measures of limitations in function or capacity as a substitute for the listings of signs and symptoms currently in use. Limitations in function offer the potential of the specificity and quantifiability required for an orderly organization and administration of disability determinations. Furthermore, they constitute more valid indicators of disability in comparison to pathology and impairment (Nagi 1979). The second direction for change is actually toward the inclusion of additional criteria — measures of physical, mental, emotional, and sensory requirements of the various jobs. The *Dictionary of Occupational Titles* (DOT) makes a very limited attempt in this direction by classifying jobs in gross categories of the types and degrees of efforts required. The need, however, is for a detailed system that identifies specific dimensions of requirements, reliable and valid measures for them, and the weights to be accorded to each.

The matching of residual capacities with work requirements not only would provide a more meaningful basis for the determination of disability but also would be of great assistance in the vocational rehabilitation and job placement of disabled beneficiaries. Such an approach to the definition of disability should be linked to an automatic filtering system into vocational counseling and rehabilitation. This should be done in such a way as to provide incentives for active participation in rehabilitation until and unless such time as a definite determination of a lack of rehabilitation and reemployment potential has been made. This would reemphasize the importance of rehabilitation and return to employment where possible, in line with concerns expressed when the merits of the SSDI program were being discussed in Congress before its passage in 1956. Such an incentive could possibly be established by making the payment of disability benefits problematic if involvement in a rehabilitation program were not maintained.

A comment must be made about the role of vocational rehabilitation. Based on the data presented here, there is a strong suggestion that the inability to get and hold a job rather than the inability to do the job may be the critical consideration in applying for SSDI benefits. Under these circumstances, what is the function of vocational rehabilitation? Is it to help the individual find and get a job, as this may require job counseling and training, or is it to restore or train to the capability to perform a job? Consideration should be given to the possibility that the former often may be much more the need than the latter even for individuals who present definite evidence of specific job-related impairments.

From the research viewpoint, change in these directions is feasible. While requiring funds, time, and effort, it is possible to develop the measures needed. Such change would require only simple alterations in the statutory language; however, program implementation would call for major alterations in the existing operations. For example, disability examiners and consultant physicians would need to be trained in the use of measures of function instead of the listings. They also would need to learn the matching of residual capacities with work requirements. Specialists in work evaluation would become part of the consultant staff, which is now made up primarily of physicians. The obsolescence such change would introduce into the present manpower and training programs would be certain to evoke strong negative reactions. The painful change in procedures and organizational structure is also bound to engender objections on the part of present-day agencies.

Barriers to Movement from and Return to the Status of a Beneficiary

As discussed, the program is operationalized now to include an earnings test of disability, "Substantial Gainful Activity" (SGA). An applicant's earnings must not equal or exceed this level in order to be eligible for disability benefits. The same criterion is applied for removing beneficiaries from that status when they have successfully completed their "trial work period" and when their earnings are equal to or greater than the SGA level. The disincentive this provision constitutes has been described earlier. Possible options include raising the level of SGA to allow beneficiaries greater incentive toward higher earnings; removing that provision in connection with the termination of benefits allowing beneficiaries to earn at higher levels, losing one dollar in taxes for every two they earn in a fashion similar to retirement benefits; or keeping the SGA but making it possible for beneficiaries whose benefits have been terminated to return to the beneficiary status without waiting periods for eligibility or for acquiring Medicare coverage when their earnings fall below the SGA level *and* as long as their limitations in capacity have not improved.

Reform has been in the direction of the first option; that is, raising the SGA level. Although this allows higher levels of earnings for beneficiaries without losing their status, it continues to lock them into the system by inhibiting attempts to exceed whatever level is specified. In other words, that option does not address the problem of incentives in a fundamental manner. The other two options that offer radical solutions to the problem of incentives require more complex recordkeeping operations. However, there is a precedent and a model of recordkeeping for the third option, which is the most complex. The model, as pointed out above, is that of the earnings of retirement insurance beneficiaries.

The Jurisdictional Question of Decision and Reviews

This issue has been the subject of repeated recommendations (Dixon 1973), most of which stem from variations among states in disability determination services. The thrust of these recommendations is to federalize the system of determinations, which is funded totally by the federal government. The object, of course, is to combine the administrative lines of authority with the technical knowledge of the Social Security Administration. The purpose would be to enhance uniformity in operations and determinations. As might be expected, the issue is highly political, involving the sensitive questions of state-federal relations. Agencies to whom the function of determinations is contracted would resent the loss of this aspect of their domains. Furthermore, the disability determination services and their personnel also would favor the status quo, which allows them the flexibility described earlier. The result is a strong coalition which objects to such a change. A statement attributed to John Gardner is appropriate here: "Organizations never die, they don't even fade away." In the quest for protecting, if not expanding, their domains and in seeking opportunities to enhance their own interests, service organizations and helping professions often ignore and sometimes even defeat change directed toward benefiting the clients for whose service they have been established.

REFERENCES

Allan, Kathryn H. 1976. "First Findings of the 1972 Survey of the Disabled: General Characteristics." *Social Security Bulletin* 39, no. 10.

____, and Cinsky, Mildred E. 1972. "General Characteristics of the Disabled Population." *Social Security Bulletin* 35 (August): 24-37.

Barker, Edward, ed. 1962. *Social Contract.* New York: Oxford University Press.

Bentley, Arthur. 1949. *The Process of Government.* Bloomington, Ind.: Principia Press.

Berkowitz, Edward. 1976. "Rehabilitation: The Federal Government's Response to Disability, 1935-54." Ph.D. dissertation, Northwestern University.

Berkowitz, Monroe, et al. 1975. *An Evaluation of Policy-Related Rehabilitation Research.* New York: Praeger.

Braybrooke, David, and Lindblom, Charles E. 1963. *A Strategy of Decisions.* New York: Free Press.

Brehm, Henry. 1970. "The Disabled on Public Assistance." *Social Security Bulletin* 33 (June): 26-30.

Burdette, Mary Ellen, and Frohlich, Phillip. 1977. "The Effect of Disability in Unit Income — 1972 Survey of Disabled and Nondisabled Adults." Social Security Administration, Office of Research and Statistics, Report no. 9.

Campbell, Susan. 1967. "A Changing Federalism: Federal-State Relations in the Disability Insurance Program." Master's Thesis, University of Massachusetts.

Cohen, Morris. 1957. *A Preface to Logic.* New York: Meridian.

Cohen, Wilbur J., and Ball, Robert M. 1968. "Social Security Amendments of 1967: Summary and Legislative History." *Social Security Bulletin* 31, no. 2.

____. 1965. "Social Security Amendments of 1965: Summary and Legislative History." *Social Security Bulletin* 28, no. 9.

133

Committee on Medical Rating of Physical Impairment. 1960. "Guides to the Evaluation of Permanent Impairment." *Journal of the American Medical Association* (March).

Connally, William. 1977. *The Public Interest.* Washington, D.C.: American Political Science Association, Division of Educational Affairs.

Consulting Group on Welfare Reform. 1977. *Report on the 1977 Welfare Reform Study,* Supplement no. 1, Secretary's Report to the President, vol. 2, HEW.

Dahl, Robert A. 1961. *Who Governs?* New Haven, Conn.: Yale University Press.

Dexter, Lewis A. 1964. *Tyranny of Schooling, An Inquiry into the Problem of Stupidity.* New York: Basic Books.

Dixon, Robert G. 1973. *Social Security Disability and Mass Justice: A Problem in Welfare Adjudication.* New York: Praeger.

Dye, Thomas R. 1972. *Understanding Public Policy.* Englewood Cliffs, N.J.: Prentice-Hall.

Eisenhower, Dwight D. 1960. *The Public Papers of the Presidents of the United States,* vol. 1954. Washington, D.C.: Government Printing Office.

Fuchs, Victor. 1974. *Who Shall Live? Health, Economics and Social Choice.* New York: Basic Books.

Furniss, Norman, and Tilton, Timothy, 1977. *The Case for the Welfare State; From Social Security to Social Equality.* Bloomington: Indiana University Press.

Galbraith, John K. 1970. *The Affluent Society.* 2d ed. New York: Penguin.

_____. 1967. *The New Industrial State.* New York: Penguin.

General Accounting Office. 1976. *Improvements Needed in Rehabilitating Social Security Disability Insurance Beneficiaries.* Report No. B-16403(4).

George, Vic, and Wilding, Paul. 1976. *Ideology and Social Welfare, Radical Social Policy.* London: Routledge and Kegan Paul.

Goff, Phoebe H. 1973. "Disabled Worker Beneficiaries Under OASDHI: Regulations and State Patterns." *Social Security Bulletin* 36 (September).

_____. 1971. "Disabled Beneficiary Population, 1957-1966." *Social Security Bulletin* 34 (July): 32-42.

Goldsborough, George J., Jr., Tinsley, William G., and Sternberg, Arnold C. 1963. *The Social Security Administration: An Inter-Disciplinary Study of Disability Evaluation, Part I: The Administrative Determination of Permanent and Total Disability.* Washington, D.C.: George Washington University.

Haber, Lawrence D. 1968. "Disability, Work, and Income Maintenance: Prevalence of Disability, 1966." *Social Security Bulletin* 31, no. 5.

_____. 1967. "Identifying the Disabled: Concepts and Methods in the Measurement of Disability." *Social Security Bulletin* 30, no. 12.

Haveman, Robert H., ed. 1977. *A Decade of Federal Anti-Poverty Programs, Achievements, Failures and Lessons.* New York: Academic Press.

Interdepartment Committee to Coordinate Health and Welfare Activities. "Message from President Transmitting the Report and Recommendations on National Health." House Document 120, 76th Congress, 1st Session, Health Security.

James, Dorothy B. 1972. *Poverty, Politics, and Change.* Englewood Cliffs, N.J.: Prentice-Hall.

Kerlinger, Fred N., and Pedhauzur, Elazar J. 1973. *Multiple Regression in the United States*. New York: Holt, Rinehart and Winston.

Keynes, John M. 1927. *The End of Laissez-Faire*. London: Hogarth.

Lindblom, Charles E. 1959. "The Science of Muddling Through." *Public Administration Review* 19.

Macarov, David. 1978. *The Design of Social Welfare*. New York: Holt, Rinehart and Winston.

Melvin, John L., and Nagi, Saad Z. 1970. "Factors in Behavioral Responses to Impairments." *Archives of Physical Medicine and Rehabilitation* 51 (September): 552-57.

Merriam, Charles. 1946. *Relief and Social Security*. Washington, D.C.: The Brookings Institution.

Mitchell, William L. 1960. "Social Security Legislation in the 86th Congress." *Social Security Bulletin* 23, no. 11.

Moore, Marjorie E., and Sanders, Barkev S. 1950. "Extent of Total Disability in the United States." *Social Security Bulletin* 13, no. 11, pp. 7-14.

Morris, Robert. 1979. *Social Policy of the American Welfare State; An Introduction to Policy Analysis*. New York: Harper & Row.

Munnell, Alicia H. 1977. *The Future of Social Security*. Washington, D.C.: The Brookings Institution.

Myrdal, Gunnar. 1976. "Race and Class in the Welfare State." Introductory lecture to a symposium in a series entitled, "The National Purpose Reconsidered: 1776-1976," Columbia University, October 28.

Nagi, Saad Z. 1979. *Disability Policies and Programs: Issues and Options*. Report to the Office of the Assistant Secretary for Planning and Evaluation, Department of Health, Education, and Welfare, Mershon Center, Ohio State University, Columbus.

_____. 1977. *Disability in the United States: A Plan for an Information System*. Report prepared for the Office for Handicapped Individuals, Office of Human Development, U.S. Department of Health, Education, and Welfare.

_____. 1976. "An Epidemiology of Disability Among Adults in the United States." *Milbank Memorial Fund Quarterly/Health and Society* 54 (Fall): 439-67.

_____. 1974. "Gatekeeping Decisions in Service Organizations." *Human Organization* 33 (Spring): 47-58.

_____. 1969a. "Congruency in Medical and Self-Assessment in Disability." *Industrial Medicine and Surgery* 38 (March): 27-36.

_____. 1969b. *Disability and Rehabilitation: Legal, Clinical, and Self-Concepts and Measurement*. Columbus: Ohio State University Press.

_____. 1965. "Some Conceptual Issues in Disability and Rehabilitation." In *Sociology and Rehabilitation*, ed. Marvin B. Sussman, pp. 100-13. Washington, D.C.: American Sociology Association.

_____. n.d. Unpublished material based on analysis of Vocational Rehabilitation Forms (R-300).

Navarro, Vincente. 1976. *Medicine Under Capitalism*. New York: Prodist.

Piven, Frances Fox, and Cloward, Richard A. 1970. *Regulating the Poor; The Function of Public Welfare*. New York: Vintage Books.

Regional SSA Program Circular. 1972. D.F. No. 72-11 (49). San Franciso. 12/6/72. "Sequential Evaluation Process in the Adjudication of Disability Claims." (An internal memo issued by the San Francisco Regional Disability Insurance Office.)

Rein, Martin. 1974. "Policy Analysis and Equality." In *Social Problems and Public Policy: Inequality and Justice,* ed. Lee Rainwater. Chicago: Aldine.

———. 1970. *Social Policy: Issues of Choice and Change.* New York: Random House.

Reisman, D. A. 1977. *Richard Titmuss, Welfare and Society.* London: Heinemann.

Report of the National Commission on State Workmen's Compensation Laws. 1972. Washington, D.C.: Government Printing Office.

Rimlinger, Gaston. 1971. *Welfare Policy and Industrialization in Europe, America, and Russia.* New York: Wiley.

Rock, Michael H. 1969. *An Evaluation of the SSA Appeals Process.* Social Security Administration, Operations Research Staff Progress Report, no. 6.

Ryan, William. 1976. *Blaming the Victim.* New York: Vintage Books.

Sanders, Barkev S., and Moore, Marjorie E. 1955. "Estimates of the Prevalence of Disability in the United States, September 1950." U.S. Department of Health, Education, and Welfare, Office of Vocational Rehabilitation, Rehabilitation Service Series, no. 317.

Schechter, Evan S. 1977. "Employment and Work Adjustments of the Disabled: 1972 Survey of Disabled and Nondisabled Adults." *Social Security Bulletin* 40, no. 7.

Schottland, Charles I. 1958. "Social Security Amendments of 1958: A Summary and Legislative History." *Social Security Bulletin* 21, no. 10.

Selye, Hans. 1956. *The Stress of Life.* New York: McGraw-Hill.

Sharkansky, Ira. 1971. "State Administrators in the Political Process." In *Politics in the American States,* ed. Herbert Jacob and Kenneth N. Vines. 2d ed. Boston: Little, Brown & Co., chap. 7.

Spreitzer, Elmer; Larson, David; and Nagi, Saad Z. 1973. *Temporary Disability Insurance in the United States.* Columbus: Mershon Center, Ohio State University.

Stevens, Robert, and Stevens, Rosemary. 1974. *Welfare Medicine in America: A Case Study of Medicaid.* New York: Free Press.

Swisher, Idella G. 1971. "Sources and Size of Income of the Disabled." Social Security Administration, Office of Research and Statistics Report, no. 16, Social Security Survey of the Disabled: 1966.

Titmuss, Richard M. 1974. *Social Policy: An Introduction.* New York: Pantheon Books.

Truman, David B. 1951. *The Governmental Process.* New York: Alfred A. Knopf.

U.S., Congress. 1952. *Congressional Record,* 98, pp. 54-56, *passim.*

U.S., Congress, House. 1973. *Compilation of the Social Security Laws,* vols. 1-2, 93rd Cong., 1st sess., Document no. 93-117.

———. 1963. "Social Security Amendments of 1963." 78th Cong., 1st sess., H. Rept. 2861.

———. 1954. "Social Security Amendments of 1954." 83rd Cong., 2d sess., H. Rept. 1698.

_____. 1943. *Security, Work, and Relief Policies,* 78th Cong., 1st sess., Document no. 128, pt. 3.

_____. 1939a. *Health Security,* 76th Cong., 1st sess., Document no. 120.

_____. 1939b. *Report of the Social Security Board to the President and to the Congress of the United States: Proposed Changes in the Social Security Act, December 30, 1938,* 76th Cong., 1st sess., Document no. 110.

_____. Committee on Ways and Means. 1974. *Committee Staff Report on the Disability Insurance Program.* Washington, D.C.: Government Printing Office.

_____. 1960. *On Administration of the Social Security Disability Insurance Program.* Washington, D.C.: Government Printing Office.

_____. 1954. *Hearings on Social Security Amendments of 1954.* 83rd Cong., 2d sess.

_____. 1949. *Minority Report to Accompany H.R. 6000,* 81st Cong., 1st sess., H. Rept. 1300.

_____. 1946. *Issues in Social Security: A Report by the Committee's Social Security Technical Staff,* 79th Cong., 1st sess.

_____. Committee on Ways and Means. Subcommittee on Social Security. 1959. *Disability Insurance Fact Book.* Washington, D.C.: Governnent Printing Office.

U.S., Congress, Senate. 1963. "Social Security Amendments of 1963." 78th Cong., 1st sess., S. Rept. 1161.

_____. 1956. "Social Security Amendments of 1956." 84th Cong., 2d sess., S. Rept. 2133.

_____. 1950. "Social Security Amendments of 1950." 81st Cong., 2d sess., S. Rept. 1669.

_____. 1948. *OASI: A Report to the Senate Committee on Finance from the Advisory Council on Social Security,* 80th Cong., 2d sess., Document no. 149.

_____. Committee on Education and Labor. 1939. *Hearings to Establish a National Health Program,* 76th Cong., 1st sess.

_____. Committee on Finance. 1955. *Hearings on the Social Security Amendments,* 84th Cong., 2d sess.

_____. 1939. *Hearings on H.R. 6655,* 76th Cong., 1st sess.

U.S., Department of Commerce, Bureau of the Census. 1973. "Characteristics of the Population, United States Summary." *1970 Census of Population,* vol. 1, pt. 1, section 2, table 205, pp. 656-57, and table 220, p. 712-17.

U.S., Department of Health, Education, and Welfare, National Center for Health Statistics. 1978. "Current Estimates, Health Interview Survey: U.S. 1977." *Vital and Health Statistics,* Series 10, no. 126 (September).

_____. 1967. "Limitation of Activity Due to Chronic Conditions." *Vital and Health Statistics,* series 10, no. 111.

_____. 1961. "Health Interview Responses Compared with Medical Records." *Health Statistics: The National Health Survey,* series D, no. 5.

U.S., Department of Health, Education, and Welfare, Social Security Administration. 1973. *Social Security Handbook.* 5th ed. DHEW Publication no. (SSA) 73-10135.

_____. 1972. *Regional SSA Program Circular.* D.F., no. 72-11-(49), S.F. 12/6/72.

———. 1970. *Disability Evaluation Under Social Security, A Handbook for Physicians.* SSI-89.

———. 1965. "Social Security Legislation in 1964." *Social Security Bulletin* 28, no. 5, pp. 24-25.

———. 1962. "News and Brief Reports." *Social Security Bulletin* 25, no. 7.

———. 1938. "Social Security in Review." *Social Security Bulletin* 1, no. 3, p. 4.

———. Federal Security Agency. 1942. *Seventh Annual Report.* Washington, D.C.: Government Printing Office.

———. Office of Research and Statistics. 1979. *Monthly Benefit Statistics,* no. 9. DHEW Publication no. (SSA) 79-11703.

Warren, Roland L. 1972. "The Concerting of Decisions as a Variable in Organizational Interaction." In *Interorganizational Decision Making,* ed. Matthew F. Tuite, Roger K. Chisholm, and Michael Radnor. Chicago: Aldine.

Weber, Max. 1949. "Objectivity in Social Science and Social Policy." In *Max Weber on the Methodology of the Social Sciences,* trans. and ed. Edward A. Shils and H. A. Finch. Glencoe, Ill.: Free Press.

Witte, Edwin. 1962. *The Development of the Social Security Act.* Madison: University of Wisconsin Press.

Wright, Deil. 1967. "Executive Leadership in State Administration." *Midwest Journal of Political Science* 11 (February).

APPENDIX A:

List of Study Variables

Variable Number	Variable Name

Social Security Administration program measures

| 1065 | Percent initial determinations 1970 are of disability-insured population, January 1971 (*applications*) |
| 1182 | Percent initial allowances are of disability-insured population, 1970 (*awards*) |

Social Security Administration administrative variables

1018	Percent of expenditures on medical exams, 1970
1019	Dollars spent per employee, 1970
1022	Nonmedical dollars spent per case completed, 1970
1028	Percent of cases completed which were initial determinations, 1970
1031	Average elapsed time for not developed cases, 1969-71
1032	Average elapsed time for developed cases, 1969-71
1033	Percent of initial allowances returned for substantive reasons, 1970
1034	Percent of initial denials returned for substantive reasons, 1970
1038	Percent allowed for listing A1, 1969
1040	Percent allowed for listings other than A1 or B1, 1969
1061	Percent of initial cases returned to state on which state agency reverses its decision from allow to deny, 1970
1079	Average salary, disability examiner, 1970

U.S. Census of Population, 1970, disability measures, general

995	Percent partially disabled
999	Percent severely disabled
1003	Percent disabled, total

U.S. Census of Population, 1970, disability measures, disaggregated

968	Percent partially disabled, males
969	Percent partially disabled, females
970	Percent severely disabled, males
971	Percent severely disabled, females
972	Percent disabled, total, males
973	Percent disabled, total, females
962	Percent partially disabled, under 55
963	Percent partially disabled, 55 and above
964	Percent severely disabled, under 55
965	Percent severely disabled, 55 and above
966	Percent disabled, total, under 55
967	Percent disabled, total, 55 and above
974	Percent partially disabled, white
975	Percent partially disabled, black
978	Percent severely disabled, white
979	Percent severely disabled, black
982	Percent disabled, total, white

Variable Number	Variable Name

U.S. Census of Population, 1970, disability measures, disaggregated (continued)

983	Percent disabled, total, black
932	Percent partially disabled, 0-8 years education
933	Percent partially disabled, 9-12 years education
934	Percent partially disabled, 13 and above years education
935	Percent severely disabled, 0-8 years education
936	Percent severely disabled, 9-12 years education
937	Percent severely disabled, 13 and above years education
938	Percent disabled, total, 0-8 years education
939	Percent disabled, total, 9-12 years education
940	percent disabled, total, 13 and above years education

U.S. Census of Population, 1970, socioeconomic characteristics

1100	Percent of families earning under $4,000, nondisabled, earner present
1103	Percent of families with social security income, nondisabled
1107	Percent males under 65 in the labor force, nondisabled
1108	Percent females under 65 in the labor force, nondisabled
1113	Percent of labor force unemployed, nondisabled
1115	Percent of labor force with less than a ninth-grade education, nondisabled
1120	Index of occupational diversity of labor force, nondisabled (inverted measure)
1121	Percent of labor force self-employed or an unpaid family worker, nondisabled
1123	Index of industrial diversity of labor force, nondisabled (inverted measure)
1125	Percent working under 15 hours a week, nondisabled

APPENDIX B:

Data Input for Each Study
Variable by State

Record	Name	995	999	1003	1065	1182
1	Maine	5.8323	3.9344	9.7667	1.1058	.0062
2	New Hampshire	4.5583	2.4328	6.9910	.8178	.0036
3	Vermont	7.0460	3.4136	10.4595	.9683	.0053
4	Massachusetts	5.2935	3.3207	8.6141	.7667	.0040
5	Rhode Island	5.2463	4.1049	9.3512	.8441	.0053
6	Connecticut	5.6288	2.5906	8.2194	.6656	.0037
7	New York	4.7768	3.7245	8.5013	.8483	.0042
8	New Jersey	4.8688	3.1755	8.0443	.8376	.0045
9	Pennsylvania	5.3040	4.1897	9.4937	.8241	.0043
10	Ohio	5.8841	3.8290	9.7131	.8479	.0041
11	Indiana	5.9084	3.6338	9.5422	.8878	.0040
12	Illinois	5.6059	3.5341	9.1400	.8106	.0039
13	Michigan	6.3854	4.0125	10.3979	1.0022	.0045
14	Wisconsin	5.9545	2.6586	8.6131	.8559	.0043
15	Minnesota	6.3489	2.6947	9.0436	.5871	.0029
16	Iowa	6.4862	2.8514	9.3376	.7435	.0045
17	Missouri	6.2852	4.5883	10.8735	.9502	.0048
18	North Dakota	5.9112	2.6127	8.5238	.8337	.0042
19	South Dakota	6.1821	3.5887	9.7708	.9786	.0049
20	Nebraska	6.3387	2.8374	9.1761	.7094	.0035
21	Kansas	6.4013	3.5840	9.9854	.8551	.0040
22	Delaware	5.5517	2.8101	8.3619	.8001	.0043
23	Maryland	5.4035	3.7070	9.1105	.9657	.0042
24	Virginia	5.2298	4.2860	9.5158	1.0733	.0039
25	West Virginia	5.9295	7.4172	13.3467	1.7387	.0076
26	North Carolina	5.8353	5.0132	10.8485	.9780	.0046

144

27	South Carolina	5.6234	6.2823	11.9057	1.2689	.0053
28	Georgia	6.7185	5.6807	12.3992	1.1300	.0050
29	Florida	6.7860	4.9098	11.6958	1.1150	.0052
30	Kentucky	5.9927	6.4050	12.3977	1.3055	.0056
31	Tennessee	5.9835	5.8754	11.8590	1.1222	.0052
32	Alabama	6.3759	5.9830	12.3590	1.4574	.0066
33	Mississippi	6.3905	7.4738	13.8644	1.7743	.0078
34	Arkansas	7.5214	6.6365	14.1579	1.7192	.0073
35	Louisiana	5.5684	6.1263	11.6947	1.6421	.0069
36	Oklahoma	7.1242	5.6652	12.7894	1.3061	.0051
37	Texas	6.0887	3.9186	10.0073	.9225	.0041
38	Montana	6.0258	3.4193	9.4451	1.1576	.0060
39	Idaho	7.7133	3.5832	11.2965	1.0059	.0049
40	Wyoming	6.5306	3.3236	9.8542	.8937	.0041
41	Colorado	6.6112	2.9498	9.5610	.9240	.0047
42	New Mexico	5.9980	4.5482	10.5462	1.2854	.0054
43	Arizona	6.5151	4.9220	11.4370	.9344	.0037
44	Utah	6.8564	2.9754	9.8318	.6524	.0035
45	Nevada	5.4599	3.1513	8.6112	.8371	.0037
46	Washington	6.8788	3.4996	10.3784	.9573	.0047
47	Oregon	7.5189	4.0676	11.5865	.9985	.0049
48	California	6.1071	4.3219	10.4290	1.1621	.0057
49	Alaska	5.0370	2.0741	7.1111	.4443	.0019
50	Hawaii	4.2138	2.9291	7.1429	.7412	.0039

Record	Name	1107	1108	1120	1123	1113	1115	1121	1125	1100
1	Maine	80.7258	47.7161	.1243	.1115	3.5623	18.6316	9.6409	22.4675	9.2473
2	New Hampshire	83.0000	55.2156	.1349	.1078	3.6120	16.8562	7.7258	20.4385	5.8020
3	Vermont	79.6834	46.4548	.1198	.0923	3.4461	17.5495	12.0613	25.6949	9.1824
4	Massachusetts	83.8873	51.5632	.1380	.0998	3.8709	15.0224	7.1967	23.6402	4.8336
5	Rhode Island	81.7276	52.3038	.1416	.1127	4.1364	20.4025	7.6300	23.1115	5.6410
6	Connecticut	84.6846	51.4595	.1379	.1217	3.5688	17.7634	7.6625	24.6080	4.1146
7	New York	81.8403	47.4937	.1387	.0891	3.9819	17.2539	8.6431	20.9390	5.0695
8	New Jersey	83.9648	48.3500	.1354	.1022	3.6851	18.5954	7.8275	216.6804	4.5063
9	Pennsylvania	82.1626	44.9555	.1307	.1084	3.5204	17.5389	7.6279	21.3350	5.6630
10	Ohio	83.4931	45.3548	.1305	.1226	3.9324	14.9402	7.3519	21.1694	5.6937
11	Indiana	83.3025	47.7039	.1276	.1282	4.1559	16.4771	8.5292	22.0040	6.9482
12	Illinois	83.4506	48.8500	.1303	.1046	3.7485	17.6237	8.3420	21.8380	5.9083
13	Michigan	82.8968	45.1516	.1326	.1388	5.4253	14.8375	7.2640	25.0637	5.1959
14	Wisconsin	82.5084	48.7301	.1187	.1062	3.7011	17.5338	11.8303	24.3060	7.2399
15	Minnesota	83.3250	49.3172	.1177	.0896	4.1826	16.5702	12.4390	25.7839	8.2030
16	Iowa	83.8674	45.6249	.1099	.0958	3.5663	15.4317	17.9306	23.2631	10.2824
17	Missouri	82.2996	47.6863	.1204	.0903	4.3628	20.2546	11.4648	21.3370	10.8678
18	North Dakota	77.2215	40.2924	.1163	.1144	5.1420	25.9060	24.3389	26.9291	14.6530
19	South Dakota	81.1466	42.9725	.1122	.1125	3.1061	22.7351	26.7903	24.4565	17.7406
20	Nebraska	83.4287	47.5187	.1099	.0945	2.7229	16.3374	19.2205	24.0343	12.5433
21	Kansas	83.0389	46.8023	.1154	.0890	3.7324	14.4450	14.9679	23.0611	11.5674
22	Delaware	82.4878	48.5034	.1344	.1058	3.8294	14.6873	7.0286	22.0948	7.5772
23	Maryland	83.6774	49.1514	.1375	.0899	3.4629	18.5643	6.6733	20.1983	6.2137
24	Virginia	80.9035	46.1339	.1265	.0893	2.6243	23.6546	7.3290	18.6472	9.9269
25	West Virginia	76.3559	32.7773	.1266	.0893	5.2326	23.4434	6.3203	16.3473	12.1751
26	North Carolina	80.6735	51.8791	.1307	.1164	3.3767	25.3327	9.5715	18.9710	14.6432

#	State									
27	South Carolina	79.5177	50.2371	.1330	.1226	3.8989	29.0133	7.9068	18.6505	15.0131
28	Georgia	81.8301	50.0528	.1222	.0940	3.0927	24.4295	8.8698	18.0859	13.7845
29	Florida	80.3391	47.1476	.1243	.0886	3.7013	19.0127	9.8044	19.1224	11.6676
30	Kentucky	77.6132	41.3926	.1184	.0903	4.2820	28.2805	10.9250	19.2749	16.2819
31	Tennessee	80.1312	46.8351	.1240	.0977	4.0796	26.3975	9.1833	17.7510	14.5774
32	Alabama	78.7757	43.8434	.1222	.0960	4.6228	22.9743	8.6786	18.5199	17.3372
33	Mississippi	73.6348	43.0456	.1144	.0908	4.6562	27.6617	10.4744	19.1427	22.9333
34	Arkansas	77.5764	44.0840	.1132	.0931	5.3045	24.2468	12.8045	20.6492	20.2539
35	Louisiana	76.7591	38.6466	.1205	.0821	5.2330	25.4501	9.6717	18.8836	15.7835
36	Oklahoma	80.9359	46.0501	.1204	.0843	4.1091	15.7795	11.6258	20.3299	13.0652
37	Texas	81.2413	45.2564	.1213	.0849	3.4058	20.3652	10.2731	19.3334	13.2123
38	Montana	79.8592	42.6552	.1106	.0966	5.8824	15.1789	17.5648	24.4108	10.6595
39	Idaho	81.2401	43.5005	.1056	.0923	4.7771	13.4156	16.2022	24.5219	12.9644
40	Wyoming	82.6727	43.8919	.1129	.0886	4.2373	14.8305	15.5085	20.7273	9.4703
41	Colorado	81.7576	47.2364	.1258	.0854	3.9945	11.7969	11.3158	21.9339	9.7748
42	New Mexico	76.2849	39.8691	.1316	.0863	5.6258	16.6561	10.8091	19.4988	14.4406
43	Arizona	79.5192	43.1917	.1254	.0863	4.0197	16.4009	8.7856	19.7115	8.9447
44	Utah	80.7569	46.0280	.1265	.0900	4.7745	7.1353	8.8594	26.2920	7.7004
45	Nevada	85.2713	48.1812	.1481	.0996	5.7100	11.4199	8.7418	18.2366	8.9159
46	Washington	83.1178	46.6939	.1245	.0932	7.5412	10.7256	9.2601	23.2601	6.7379
47	Oregon	81.7314	46.2667	.1176	.0913	5.8793	11.6297	11.9520	22.5018	7.9837
48	California	82.8931	48.3118	.1300	.0891	6.0675	11.6722	9.0293	20.3928	7.1334
49	Alaska	76.8421	44.3337	.1352	.1024	9.2238	13.8358	6.6367	21.4013	8.8652
50	Hawaii	79.7160	50.0444	.1300	.0903	3.2444	17.0512	6.2725	18.5769	5.3324

Record	Name	1103	1018	1019	1022	1031	1032	1033	1061
1	Maine	21.2106	37.6142	15634.9206	27.1123	7.0000	41.6667	9.6000	58.3333
2	New Hampshire	18.2680	25.5481	14463.4146	29.8917	6.6667	46.0000	5.9000	52.3077
3	Vermont	20.0924	23.3748	11476.1905	28.1504	.6667	14.3333	9.0000	63.1579
4	Massachusetts	20.6288	33.3526	16789.4737	41.0226	1.6667	48.6667	4.3000	61.1570
5	Rhode Island	22.3657	26.7684	16794.8718	38.0487	11.0000	49.6667	9.1000	68.7500
6	Connecticut	18.7731	23.6080	13524.0964	32.3371	17.6667	59.6667	10.0000	62.5954
7	New York	19.6451	14.0039	14891.4616	45.7271	5.3333	27.3333	5.2000	52.9265
8	New Jersey	19.3150	30.6456	15505.6180	38.0168	11.0000	32.0000	7.2000	57.6000
9	Pennsylvania	20.6519	44.9591	17838.9513	27.7983	2.6667	57.0000	5.5000	65.2751
10	Ohio	17.3976	28.4566	15712.1495	30.5948	20.3333	58.0000	5.1000	54.9815
11	Indiana	17.0543	48.1441	16493.7163	20.7609	8.0000	53.3333	7.7000	49.8978
12	Illinois	17.8893	34.0018	15933.4955	30.4581	13.3333	46.0000	6.6000	56.0669
13	Michigan	17.3545	40.7282	19979.1667	32.3592	4.6667	51.3333	10.4000	52.9321
14	Wisconsin	20.5062	29.6296	18056.6038	35.2917	11.6667	52.0000	6.2000	49.2891
15	Minnesota	19.7755	24.4660	18926.5537	41.7797	17.0000	49.6667	4.0000	58.5586
16	Iowa	20.9694	34.0575	15490.3846	33.0374	2.0000	33.6667	7.0000	53.5714
17	Missouri	20.8025	32.5675	17237.6238	33.9601	8.0000	29.0000	6.6000	56.9672
18	North Dakota	20.2381	16.9756	11388.8889	38.6642	5.0000	36.6667	6.8000	64.2857
19	South Dakota	21.5970	16.6811	13541.1765	38.1768	2.3333	23.3333	5.8000	70.0000
20	Nebraska	19.6916	25.5561	12885.3503	28.6966	4.6667	37.0000	8.8000	59.3407
21	Kansas	20.2172	33.5216	18178.5714	34.9561	2.6667	35.6667	3.5000	35.8491
22	Delaware	18.6411	18.7845	12928.5714	40.5331	11.3333	32.3333	6.8000	57.8947
23	Maryland	15.4332	45.5742	18902.4390	26.5567	3.3333	41.3333	6.7000	46.5021
24	Virginia	15.8446	36.9850	15620.4620	29.4859	3.3333	43.0000	5.3000	51.0373
25	West Virginia	22.2667	49.1593	19366.6667	30.6905	3.6667	49.0000	10.8000	56.6474
26	North Carolina	17.0047	31.4169	14959.1195	26.8243	5.6667	39.3333	5.8000	46.3918

27	South Carolina	15.8420	23.0671	15676.0000	39.7129	3.6667	28.6667	5.5000	49.0446
28	Georgia	14.7909	40.4915	18737.7049	28.0435	.6667	26.0000	7.6000	48.8449
29	Florida	27.4717	36.8942	15987.8296	31.1752	1.0000	25.3333	4.8000	54.6341
30	Kentucky	21.1816	42.8796	16247.0588	28.4128	2.6667	37.3333	7.1000	53.3333
31	Tennessee	19.4249	42.9188	17780.3838	22.6775	.6667	30.3333	5.3000	53.4722
32	Alabama	18.9982	42.4527	17734.5679	23.3247	4.3333	29.0000	8.7000	48.5185
33	Mississippi	19.0371	34.2016	15693.4307	28.8550	1.0000	28.3333	10.5000	51.6393
34	Arkansas	21.7278	36.2113	16147.0588	26.3983	6.6667	24.3333	6.6000	48.9933
35	Louisiana	15.7243	43.0506	19729.6875	33.4418	1.0000	30.0000	8.2000	49.8084
36	Oklahoma	19.2415	32.0311	14032.9949	26.8065	4.6667	30.3333	7.3000	50.2110
37	Texas	16.3341	30.4426	14515.5148	30.8078	1.6667	30.0000	6.3000	46.3295
38	Montana	19.0678	34.5725	16469.3878	30.3885	7.6667	35.0000	8.1000	74.4186
39	Idaho	18.6975	33.1307	16958.7629	32.3625	1.6667	32.0000	10.5000	56.0000
40	Wyoming	15.6573	18.5529	13146.3415	32.4944	2.3333	25.6667	6.2000	66.6667
41	Colorado	15.7731	32.5000	16275.8621	36.9348	5.0000	52.3333	7.9000	50.7937
42	New Mexico	14.8718	35.0114	20125.0000	41.7910	9.3333	37.0000	7.3000	54.3478
43	Arizona	19.1598	35.7344	15922.4490	32.6602	16.0000	44.6667	7.4000	54.0541
44	Utah	15.6174	29.7480	18077.7778	41.6242	5.3333	43.6667	6.8000	41.6667
45	Nevada	10.0096	29.6356	17898.5507	37.7007	13.6667	43.6667	14.1000	51.5152
46	Washington	16.5334	36.3154	18300.0000	28.6930	3.0000	33.6667	4.4000	51.4563
47	Oregon	19.4175	29.1608	16055.1948	34.2090	9.6667	35.0000	5.2000	62.8571
48	California	16.0289	27.2810	17608.6219	34.6537	1.6667	30.6667	9.6000	53.5745
49	Alaska	5.8319	15.2778	18580.6452	80.0000	8.0000	39.3333	11.3000	83.3333
50	Hawaii	13.5117	18.0941	15942.3077	52.8816	10.0000	39.3333	7.6000	71.4286

Record	Name	1034	1028	1038	1079	1040
1	Maine	4.7000	68.2550	49.7010	6916.0000	16.1462
2	New Hampshire	8.6000	67.3324	39.4977	7450.0000	16.8950
3	Vermont	4.2000	68.3435	46.1078	7696.0000	25.0000
4	Massachusetts	2.3000	70.1432	45.0925	7784.5000	11.2272
5	Rhode Island	3.5000	68.7203	47.6904	7930.0000	10.6397
6	Connecticut	6.7000	67.1161	52.8103	10000.0000	8.3310
7	New York	4.1000	71.5530	39.9686	8552.5000	11.0351
8	New Jersey	4.6000	70.1621	36.5350	8789.0000	15.0391
9	Pennsylvania	5.1000	68.3293	46.5549	8209.0000	19.3797
10	Ohio	3.4000	69.4855	31.1261	8632.0000	22.8091
11	Indiana	9.4000	67.2114	47.0397	8370.0000	8.1060
12	Illinois	4.8000	69.3775	42.0808	8430.0000	13.1069
13	Michigan	5.4000	68.9786	41.5323	9926.5000	16.7179
14	Wisconsin	4.8000	68.7609	22.3447	9732.0000	20.2554
15	Minnesota	4.0000	66.5282	45.0696	9930.0000	16.0446
16	Iowa	3.3000	70.7344	43.0857	9214.0000	16.5130
17	Missouri	4.2000	69.0387	42.8732	9678.0000	21.3523
18	North Dakota	5.4000	62.6533	52.5358	9000.0000	22.1066
19	South Dakota	3.6000	65.4857	41.5049	9894.0000	19.9029
20	Nebraska	7.1000	64.1768	34.6893	0.0000	13.4463
21	Kansas	3.4000	70.2479	46.6435	7638.0000	14.0432
22	Delaware	4.1000	67.8768	42.6250	10800.0000	14.1250
23	Maryland	6.2000	67.5691	43.4741	9586.5000	13.9620
24	Virginia	5.1000	68.0079	41.9896	8232.0000	31.5695
25	West Virginia	6.9000	61.4218	26.5149	8400.0000	27.1061
26	North Carolina	4.5000	68.9702	46.9967	7914.0000	14.7492

27	South Carolina	3.7000	65.0685	38.2039	8387.5000	13.8835
28	Georgia	5.0000	64.5915	44.3469	9516.0000	19.4288
29	Florida	2.7000	66.0451	48.0091	8832.0000	14.2265
30	Kentucky	4.8000	64.1133	41.2578	8424.0000	30.9545
31	Tennessee	2.7000	67.2415	44.9393	9050.0000	15.5142
32	Alabama	4.3000	64.1712	39.6262	8940.0000	23.4717
33	Mississippi	5.9000	63.9720	31.2857	8500.0000	31.9762
34	Arkansas	4.0000	64.9932	30.4021	6996.0000	25.1621
35	Louisiana	4.2000	65.1770	38.9974	8750.0000	21.0717
36	Oklahoma	5.3000	65.6894	18.6528	6900.0000	26.8135
37	Texas	4.1000	65.6374	48.2138	10968.0000	18.5884
38	Montana	4.1000	63.8273	43.3995	8310.0000	20.7938
39	Idaho	6.6000	60.3413	47.7413	9858.0000	18.8912
40	Wyoming	4.3000	67.8016	26.7857	9150.0000	21.8750
41	Colorado	5.5000	65.2794	44.8605	8472.0000	15.8590
42	New Mexico	3.0000	63.3382	48.1509	8610.0000	19.0189
43	Arizona	4.7000	64.4346	45.8494	8000.0000	18.0019
44	Utah	3.0000	67.6621	43.9224	8898.0000	9.2952
45	Nevada	8.7000	57.9610	48.6862	9581.5000	22.5657
46	Washington	3.1000	69.5765	42.8540	9324.0000	19.9249
47	Oregon	4.5000	64.5508	33.9398	8646.0000	12.3770
48	California	4.6000	64.0280	33.9399	10398.0000	25.2392
49	Alaska	5.3000	71.9672	40.5530	14964.0000	23.5023
50	Hawaii	2.9000	67.4844	53.6532	9834.0000	13.4133

APPENDIX C:

Multiple Regressions, U.S. Census of
Population, 1970: Disaggregated
Disability Measures (Self-defined)
and Socioeconomic Characteristics

Stepwise Multiple Regression State Self-Defined, Percent Partially Disabled, 0-8 Years Education (932), and Socioeconomic Characteristics

Variable Number	Beta	F-Test	Multiple R^2
1120	−.5702	9.5446[a]	.4540
1125	.4175	4.918[b]	.5495
1121	−.3008	2.3863	.5625
1115	−.1904	.9249	.5692
1100	.4655	3.9839	.5897
1103	.1899	2.3088	.6117
1107	.2361	1.2886	.6286
1113	.1260	.7630	.6339
1108	.0638	.1669	.6356
1123	−.0471	.1229	.6368

[a]Significant at .01 level.
[b]Significant at .05 level.

Stepwise Multiple Regression State Self-Defined, Percent Partially Disabled, 9-12 Years Education (933), and Socioeconomic Characteristics

Variable Number	Beta	F-Test	Multiple R^2
1115	−.8263	35.9721[a]	.3045
1120	−.4904	14.5736[a]	.6087
1100	.9199	32.1211[a]	.6522
1121	−.6485	22.8963[a]	.6983
1107	.5140	12.6041[a]	.7585
1103	.1999	5.2822[b]	.7939
1125	.2736	4.3598[b]	.8152
1108	−.1091	1.0084	.8220
1113	.0662	.4343	.8238
1123	−.0221	.0559	.8241

[a]Significant at .01 level.
[b]Significant at .05 level.

Stepwise Multiple Regression State Self-Defined, Percent Partially Disabled, 13 and Above Years Education (934), and Socioeconomic Characteristics

Variable Number	Beta	F-Test	Multiple R^2
1113	.0973	.3867	.1470
1120	−.0419	.0403	.2473
1115	−.8843	18.9920*	.3536
1100	.7475	9.9475*	.4670
1103	.1686	1.4259	.4907
1108	−.1772	1.3616	.5034
1121	−.2286	1.2707	.5142
1123	.0771	.2791	.5204
1125	.0628	.0988	.5216

*Significant at .01 level.

Stepwise Multiple Regression State Self-Defined, Percent Severely Disabled, 0-8 Years Education (935), and Socioeconomic Characteristics

Variable Number	Beta	F-Test	Multiple R^2
1125	−.1003	.4122	.2542
1108	−.3060	4.4556[a]	.3629
1121	−.8714	23.2066[b]	.3990
1100	.8165	14.1670[b]	.5367
1120	−.2310	1.9949	.5908
1107	.2274	1.5059	.6190
1103	.2643	5.2004[a]	.6360
1125	−.1003	.4122	.6360
1115	−.2884	3.1989	.6751
1113	.0694	.2735	.6773

[a]Significant at .01 level.
[b]Significant at .05 level.

155

Stepwise Multiple Regression State Self-Defined, Percent Severely Disabled, 9-12 Years Education (936), and Socioeconomic Characteristics

Variable Number	Beta	F-Test	Multiple R^2
1100	.8420	12.7693[a]	.2392
1121	−.4772	5.8831[b]	.3829
1103	.5375	18.1180[a]	.5040
1115	−.4259	4.5347[b]	.5814
1125	−.2535	1.7768	.6084
1108	−.1444	.8382	.6209
1120	.0743	.1587	.6245
1113	.0791	.2942	.6268
1107	.0723	.1182	.6287
1123	.0332	.0597	.6293

[a]Significant at .01 level.
[b]Significant at .05 level.

Stepwise Multiple Regression State Self-Defined, Percent Severely Disabled, 13 and Above Years Education (937), and Socioeconomic Characteristics

Variable Number	Beta	F-Test	Multiple R^2
1100	.7552	8.8895[a]	.2447
1115	−.4659	4.6954[b]	.2883
1125	−.4973	5.9165[b]	.3413
1103	.4736	12.1696[a]	.4379
1120	.4752	5.6200[b]	.4750
1121	.4042	3.6532	.5368
1113	.2183	1.9421	.5603
1107	.2193	.9424	.5665
1108	−.1120	.4361	.5713
1123	−.0204	.0195	.5716

[a]Significant at .01 level.
[b]Significant at .05 level.

Stepwise Multiple Regression State Self-Defined, Percent Disabled, Total, 0-8 Years Education (938), and Socioeconomic Characteristics

Variable Number	Beta	F-Test	Multiple R^2
1100	.8734	13.0602[a]	.2299
1115	−.3268	2.5375	.2902
1121	−.8342	17.0905[a]	.3612
1120	−.4686	6.0014[b]	.5121
1103	.3029	5.4690[b]	.5770
1108	−.2083	1.6581	.5861
1107	.2930	1.8481	.5965
1113	.1161	.6032	.6054
1125	.1243	.4061	.6098
1123	−.0160	.0133	.6100

[a]Significant at .01 level.
[b]Significant at .05 level.

Stepwise Multiple Regression State Self-Defined, Percent Disabled, Total, 9-12 Years Education (939), and Socioeconomic Characteristics

Variable Number	Beta	F-Test	Multiple R^2
1120	−.2837	3.2475	.1606
1121	−.7210	17.1454[a]	.2598
1115	−.8062	26.9809[a]	.3351
1100	1.1207	28.8045[a]	.5119
1103	.4544	16.5844[a]	.6631
1107	.3911	4.8050[b]	.6822
1108	−.1598	1.3107	.6958
1113	.0924	.5232	.7006
1125	.0361	.0577	.7010

[a]Significant at .01 level.
[b]Significant at .05 level.

Stepwise Multiple Regression State Self-Defined, Percent Disabled, Total, 13 and Above Years Education (940), and Socioeconomic Characteristics

Variable Number	Beta	F-Test	Multiple R^2
1108	−.1766	1.0530	.1502
1115	−.8918	16.7109[a]	.2676
1100	.8628	11.2679[a]	.4903
1103	.3018	4.8007[b]	.5106
1120	.1279	.3955	.5398
1113	.1511	.9034	.5482
1125	−.1255	.3659	.5552
1123	.0595	.1613	.5580
1107	.0570	.0619	.5584
1121	−.0413	.0371	.5588

[a]Significant at .01 level.
[b]Significant at .05 level.

Stepwise Multiple Regression State Self-Defined, Percent Partially Disabled, Under 55 (962), and Socioeconomic Characteristics

Variable Number	Beta	F-Test	Multiple R^2
1120	−.4704	9.8473[a]	.2561
1115	−.6791	21.1057[a]	.3958
1100	1.1003	30.6112[a]	.4906
1121	−.7851	22.4108[a]	.5713
1103	.2851	7.1959[b]	.6414
1125	.3481	5.9099[b]	.6774
1107	.4247	6.2479[b]	.7141
1113	.1516	1.5523	.7278
1108	−.0509	.1465	.7288

[a]Significant at .01 level.
[b]Significant at .05 level.

Stepwise Multiple Regression State Self-Defined, Percent Partially Disabled, 55 and Above (963), and Socioeconomic Characteristics

Variable Number	Beta	F-Test	Multiple R^2
1120	−.4442	5.6249[a]	.4093
1113	.1597	1.1899	.5091
1100	.7567	10.2251[b]	.5316
1115	−.2379	1.4034	.5769
1123	.0453	.1103	.5908
1107	.2916	1.9094	.5949
1125	.2859	2.2396	.5986
1121	−.2715	1.8889	.6096
1108	−.1709	1.1646	.6183
1103	−.1128	.7909	.6261

[a]Significant at .01 level.
[b]Significant at .05 level.

Stepwise Multiple Regression State Self-Defined, Percent Severely Disabled, Under 55 (964), and Socioeconomic Characteristics

Variable Number	Beta	F-Test	Multiple R^2
1115	.2135	2.9554	.4665
1125	−.1630	1.9046	.6049
1108	−.2797	8.1512*	.6975
1100	.6478	19.5927*	.7269
1121	−.5280	18.6734*	.8021
1103	.2630	11.2447*	.8471
1107	.1568	1.4428	.8514
1113	.1010	1.2442	.8567
1123	.0242	.0824	.8569
1120	−.0126	.0118	.8570

*Significant at .01 level.

159

Stepwise Multiple Regression State Self-Defined, Percent Severely Disabled, 55 and Above (965), and Socioeconomic Characteristics

Variable Number	Beta	F-Test	Multiple R^2
1125	−.2385	3.5718	.4883
1100	.7100	20.6284[a]	.6584
1121	−.7025	28.9677[a]	.7776
1103	.1709	4.1615[b]	.8047
1108	−.1491	2.0299	.8183
1120	−.1845	2.2245	.8241
1123	.0646	.5137	.8296
1107	.1463	1.1010	.8324
1113	.0971	1.0088	.8358
1115	.0643	.2351	.8368

[a]Significant at .01 level.
[b]Significant at .05 level.

Stepwise Multiple Regression State Self-Defined, Percent Disabled, Total, Under 55 (966), and Socioeconomic Characteristics

Variable Number	Beta	F-Test	Multiple R^2
1100	1.0904	40.2121[a]	.4553
1121	−.8304	33.4526[a]	.5735
1120	−.2558	3.5338	.6560
1103	.3584	15.1223[a]	.7027
1115	−.1848	1.6032	.7508
1108	−.2493	4.6923[b]	.7670
1107	.3463	5.0984[b]	.7860
1113	.1595	2.2477	.8009
1125	.0514	.1372	.8023
1123	.0199	.0404	.8025

[a]Significant at .01 level.
[b]Significant at .05 level.

Stepwise Multiple Regression State Self-Defined, Percent Disabled, Total, 55 and Above (967), and Socioeconomic Characteristics

Variable Number	Beta	F-Test	Multiple R^2
1100	.9116	23.5740[a]	.5200
1121	−.6897	19.3565[a]	.6602
1120	−.3471	5.4542[b]	.7132
1108	−.1968	2.4516	.7297
1107	.2482	2.1970	.7463
1113	.1497	1.6611	.7573
1103	.0882	.7689	.7617
1123	.0725	.4482	.7631
1125	−.0660	.1894	.7639
1115	−.0538	.1137	.7646

[a]Significant at .01 level.
[b]Significant at .05 level.

Stepwise Multiple Regression State Self-Defined, Percent Partially Disabled, Males (968), and Socioeconomic Characteristics

Variable Number	Beta	F-Test	Multiple R^2
1120	−.4488	11.5238[a]	.5453
1113	.1992	3.7159	.6235
1103	.2422	7.3188[a]	.6501
1100	.8976	28.8736[a]	.6662
1115	−.3908	7.5967[a]	.7567
1121	−.4448	10.1708[a]	.7716
1125	.3125	5.3709[b]	.7868
1107	.3251	4.7615[b]	.7968
1108	−.2053	3.3697	.8129
1123	−.0377	.1529	.8137

[a]Significant at .01 level.
[b]Significant at .05 level.

Stepwise Multiple Regression State Self-Defined, Percent Partially Disabled, Females (969), and Socioeconomic Characteristics

Variable Number	Beta	F-Test	Multiple R^2
1120	−.4031	3.5745	.1082
1115	−.5914	6.6895[a]	.1868
1121	−.7305	10.5479[b]	.2393
1100	1.0613	15.5193[b]	.2874
1107	.5439	5.1241[a]	.4338
1103	.2373	2.7001	.4810
1125	.2129	.9589	.5115
1123	.0774	.2487	.5147
1108	.0403	.0499	.5152
1113	.0185	.0123	.5154

[a]Significant at .01 level.
[b]Significant at .05 level.

Stepwise Multiple Regression State Self-Defined, Percent Severely Disabled, Males (970), and Socioeconomic Characteristics

Variable Number	Beta	F-Test	Multiple R^2
1107	.0362	.1199	.4935
1125	−.2298	6.8141[a]	.6773
1103	.2958	20.5007[b]	.7834
1100	.4933	16.2756[b]	.8129
1121	−.4389	18.5291[b]	.8427
1108	−.2786	11.6233[b]	.8814
1115	.2058	5.1264[a]	.8885
1113	.1354	3.2786	.8962
1120	−.0634	.4736	.8975

[a]Significant at .01 level.
[b]Significant at .05 level.

Stepwise Multiple Regression State Self-Defined, Percent Severely Disabled, Females (971), and Socioeconomic Characteristics

Variable Number	Beta	F-Test	Multiple R^2
1125	−.1976	2.1005	.3934
1100	.7948	22.1433[a]	.5701
1121	−.6951	24.2959[a]	.6605
1103	.3388	14.0058[a]	.7707
1107	.3134	4.3292[b]	.7770
1108	−.1800	2.5352	.7966
1123	.0723	.5517	.8013
1120	−.1234	.8516	.8044
1113	.0986	.8905	.8069
1115	.1031	.5167	.8095

[a]Significant at .01 level.
[b]Significant at .05 level.

Stepwise Multiple Regression State Self-Defined, Percent Disabled, Total, Males (972), and Socioeconomic Characteristics

Variable Number	Beta	F-Test	Multiple R^2
1100	.8217	47.7581[a]	.6068
1108	−.3045	13.2130[a]	.6879
1121	−.5433	35.9523[a]	.7323
1103	.3379	24.0870[a]	.8046
1120	−.2829	7.7233[a]	.8401
1113	.2019	6.1243[b]	.8634
1107	.1969	3.1449	.8770
1115	−.0619	.3418	.8788
1123	−.0203	.0883	.8791

[a]Significant at .01 level.
[b]Significant at .05 level.

Stepwise Multiple Regression State Self-Defined, Percent Disabled, Total, Females (973), and Socioeconomic Characteristics

Variable Number	Beta	F-Test	Multiple R^2
1100	1.0470	24.1576[a]	.2949
1121	−.8421	22.4138[a]	.4801
1103	.3661	10.2841[a]	.5849
1107	.4596	5.8514[b]	.6368
1120	−.2513	2.2223	.6645
1108	−.1326	.8642	.6819
1113	.0877	.4432	.6911
1115	−.1359	.5648	.6926
1123	.0882	.5152	.6951
1125	−.0826	.2310	.6970

[a]Significant at .01 level.
[b]Significant at .05 level.

Stepwise Multiple Regression State Self-Defined, Percent Partially Disabled, White (974), and Socioeconomic Characteristics

Variable Number	Beta	F-Test	Multiple R^2
1120	−.5235	9.3663[a]	.4350
1115	−.5193	8.0154[a]	.5172
1100	.8256	14.5958[a]	.5950
1103	.2167	3.5005	.6235
1121	−.4212	5.4495[b]	.6462
1125	.2031	1.3557	.6575
1107	.3254	2.8500	.6731
1113	.1600	1.4334	.6873
1108	−.0422	.0852	.6880
1123	−.0157	.0159	.6881

[a]Significant at .01 level.
[b]Significant at .05 level.

Stepwise Multiple Regression State Self-Defined, Percent Partially Disabled, Black (975), and Socioeconomic Characteristics

Variable Number	Beta	F-Test	Multiple R^2
1107	−.5059	3.2268	.0958
1115	−.8012	8.9348[a]	.1971
1123	.3913	4.6208[b]	.2178
1100	.3136	.9863	.2463
1113	−.1766	.8175	.2661
1121	−.2784	1.1148	.2872
1120	−.2737	1.1990	.3138
1108	−.1057	.2501	.3250
1125	−.1671	.4296	.3304
1103	.0779	.2118	.3341

[a]Significant at .01 level.
[b]Significant at .05 level.

Stepwise Multiple Regression State Self-Defined, Percent Severely Disabled, White (978), and Socioeconomic Characteristics

Variable Number	Beta	F-Test	Multiple R^2
1100	.6119	16.6850[a]	.4012
1121	−.5212	17.3591[a]	.6299
1103	.4312	28.8387[a]	.7717
1108	−.2280	5.1686[b]	.8101
1125	−.2864	5.6097[b]	.8397
1107	.1354	1.0270	.8428
1113	.0997	1.1581	.8458
1115	.0654	.2647	.8480
1120	−.0783	.4363	.8491
1123	.0439	.2585	.8501

[a]Significant at .01 level.
[b]Significant at .05 level.

Stepwise Multiple Regression State Self-Defined, Percent Severely Disabled, Black (979), and Socioeconomic Characteristics

Variable Number	Beta	F-Test	Multiple R^2
1107	−.6005	9.5655*	.3952
1120	−.6972	16.3782*	.4662
1125	−.7477	18.1062*	.6075
1100	−.3764	2.9901	.6426
1123	.2455	3.8286	.6663
1115	−.1616	.7652	.6764
1103	.0886	.5773	.6792
1113	.0814	.3655	.6818
1121	.0815	.2012	.6831
1108	.0334	.0524	.6836

*Significant at .01 level.

Stepwise Multiple Regression State Self-Defined, Percent Disabled, Total, White (982), and Socioeconomic Characteristics

Variable Number	Beta	F-Test	Multiple R^2
1100	.8591	20.0922[a]	.4430
1103	.4345	17.8932[a]	.5157
1121	−.5997	14.0451[a]	.6161
1115	−.1925	1.3998	.6797
1120	−.3055	4.0550[b]	.7078
1108	−.1959	2.3313	.7245
1107	.2569	2.2582	.7411
1113	.1519	1.6424	.7502
1125	−.1262	.6657	.7543
1123	.0266	.0578	.7547

[a]Significant at .01 level.
[b]Significant at .05 level.

Stepwise Multiple Regression State Self-Defined, Percent Disabled, Total, Black (983), and Socioeconomic Characteristics

Variable Number	Beta	F-Test	Multiple R^2
1107	−.6957	10.9671*	.3543
1120	−.6180	10.9925*	.4105
1121	−.1154	.3444	.4641
1115	−.5893	8.6909*	.4875
1125	−.5863	9.5111*	.5389
1123	.3960	8.5059*	.6155
1103	.1046	.6870	.6269
1113	−.0539	.1371	.6280
1108	−.0423	.0719	.6291
1100	−.0547	.0539	.6296

*Significant at .01 level.

INDEX

administration: disability determination process, 114-15, 116-17; influence upon social programs, 19-21; judgment regarding disability determination, 94-100

advisory council, Social Security, 55-56, 58-59, 60, 61, 65

agency efficiency, 102-3, 104-9, 115

agency expenditures, 102-3, 104-9

agency judiciousness, 102-3, 104-9

Aid to Dependent Children (ADC), 52, 53, 59

Aid to Families with Dependent Children (AFDC), 14

Aid to the Blind (AB), 52, 53, 59

Aid to the Permanently and Totally Disabled (APTD), 53, 59, 60

Altmeyer, Arthur J., 56, 60

American Medical Association, establishment of disability insurance, 60; impairments, 119-20

analytic technique: problem policy program model, 3-5; relationship between problem, policy, program in disability, 21, 25-26

anti-collectivists: disability insurance, 51, 52, 53-54, 55, 60-62, 65-66, 124; problem definition, 11

application rates, 80-84; disability benefits, 28, 112-13; professionalism, 104-9; state characteristics, 79-81

award rates, 80-84; professionalism, 106-9; state characteristics, 79-80

black lung, 13

Borderline Allowance Rate, 102, 103-9, 115

Bureau of Old Age and Survivor's Insurance, 57-58, 65

census, U.S., 1970, 26-27, 37-38, 69-71

Committee on Economic Security, 54-55

Committee on Long-Range Work and Relief Policies, 57

Committee Staff Report on Disability Insurance Program, 28

Connally, William, 7

decisions, reliability, 128-29; routinization, 128-29

depression, 51

Dexter, Anthony, 13

Dictionary of Occupational Titles, 130

disability: American Medical Association, 119-20; anti-collectivists, 124; continuum, 121-22; income and earnings, 48-49; impact, 41, 45-48; impairment, 31-32, 113-14, 119-20; knowledge about, 125-26; labor market, 110-11, 112-13; misdefined, 111-12; prevalence and incidence, 34-45; reluctant collectivists, 124; unemployment, 118-19; values, 126-27

disability determination, 125; administration, 88-109, 113, 114-15; continuum, 121-22; criteria, 130-31; dichotomy, 121-22; Disability Determining Services (DDS), 101-4, 116-17, 127; disabled-non-disabled, 121-22; Dixon, Robert G., 92, 94; guidelines, 89-94, 101-10; legislative intent, 101-9; medical

impairments, 113-14; medical profession, 121; professionalism, 101-9, 114-15; rehabilitation, 117-18; routinization, 129
disability freeze, 60-61, 63-64
disability, impairments, 113-14, 119-21
disability insurance: Altmeyer, Arthur, 56, 60; American Medical Association, 60; anti-collectivists, 51, 52, 53-54, 55, 60-62, 65-66; Bureau of Old Age Survivor's Insurance, 57-58, 65; Committee on Economic Security, 54-55; Committee on Long-Range Work and Relief Policies, 57; disability freeze, 60, 61, 62-63; Douglas, Paul, 56; establishment of, 50-67; Interdepartmental Committee to Coordinate Health and Welfare Activities, 55; *Kerner* v. *Flemming*, 64, 66; Linton, Arthur M., 56; reluctant collectivists, 50, 52; Wagner, Robert F., 56-57 (*see also* Social Security Disability Insurance)
disability, self-defined: census, U.S., 1970, 68-71; disaggregated categories, 74-75; implications, 75-76; never-worked population, 75; socioeconomic conditions, 26, 71-74, 110-11, 112, 114
disabled-non disabled dichotomy and disability determination, 121-22
disaggregated categories, self-defined disability, 74-75
Dixon, Robert G., 94
Douglas, Paul, 56
Dye, Thomas, 128

Elizabethian poor laws, 51

federalization of disability insurance administration, 132
Furniss, Norman, 7-8

Gardner, John, 132

gross national product, 1

history: disability insurance, 50-67; social problems, 11-12; Titmus, Richard, 11-12
House Ways and Means Committee, 1940, disability rates and state characteristics, 78

impairments: American Medical Association, 119-20; disability, 23, 113-14, 119-21; routinization (of disability determination), 129
incrementalism, 128; Lindblom, Charles E., 128
individualism: affect upon social problem definition, 8-10; Friedman, Milton, 8; Hayek, F.A., 8; Locke, John, 50
Interdepartmental Committee to Coordinate Health and Welfare Activities, 1937, 55, 64-66
interest groups and disability insurance, 127-28

Kerner v. *Flemming*, 64, 66

labor market and disability, 111, 112-13
legislative intent: administrative guidelines, 89-94, 100-1; social programs, 17-19
Lindblom, Charles E., 128
Linton, Arthur M., 56
Locke, John, 50

marijuana, 14
Medicaid, 54, 63
medical profession and disability determination, 121
Medicare, 52, 54, 63
methodology: data development, 22-30; identification of problem, 22-24; model analysis, 25-26; policy formulation and program development, 24-25; sources and use of data, 26-29

multi-faceted approaches, social problems, 19
Myrdal, Gunnar, 8

Nagi, Saad, 23, 31, 125, 128, 130
National Center for Health Statistics, 23, 27
Navarro, Vicente, 7
never-worked population, self-defined, 75

Old Age and Survivor's Insurance (OASI), 62
Old Age Assistance (OAA), 53, 59

pathology, disability determination, 23, 121
perspectives, social problem definition, 12-14; black lung, 13; marijuana, 14
policy formulation process, 16-17
prevalence, disability determination, 23, 34-35
problem and policy (the fit between), 84-87
professionalism: agency efficiency, 102; agency expenditures, 102-3, 105-9; agency judiciousness, 102, 103, 105-9; application rates, 105-9; award rates, 106-9; Borderline Allowance Rates, 102, 104-9, 115; disability determination, 101-9, 114-15; Disability Determination Services (DDS), 101-4; Sharkansky, Ira, 102; Wright, Deil, 103

rehabilitation: disability determination, 117-18; services, 116; vocational, 131
Rein, Martin, 7
Reisman, David, 7
reluctant collectivists: disability insurance, 50-52; Galbraith, J.K., 8-9; Keynes, J.M., 8-9; social problems, 8-11
resources and competing goals, influences on social policy, 15-16

Sharkansky, Ira, 102
social policy: definition, 5; competing goals, 15-16; factors influencing, 14-17; implications of, 5-6; limited resources, 15-16; policy formulation process, 16-17; relationship to social problems, 5-6
social problems: definition, 5; history, 11-13; nature, 13-16; values 6-11, 126-27
social programs: administrative decision-making, 19-21; factors influencing, 17-21; legislative intent, 17-19; multi-faceted approaches, 19
Social Security Act, 51-54
Social Security Board, 55-56
Social Security Disability Insurance (SSDI), 24, 34; application rates, 79-84; award rates, 79-84; change and development, 130; comparisons with other programs, 122-24; determination criteria, 130-31; federalization, 130-31; House Ways and Means Committee, 1960, 78; Gardner, John, 130-31; objectives, 129; problem and policy fit, 84-87; rehabilitation (vocational), 130-31; substantial gainful activity (SGA), 131-32 (see also disability insurance)
social welfare programs: complexity, 1-4; costs, 1, 2-3; coverage, 2-3
socioeconomic conditions and disability, 26, 71-74, 110-112, 114
substantial gainful activity (SGA), 111, 113, 122, 131-32
Supplemental Security Income (SSI), 52; compared to Social Security Disability Insurance (SSDI), 123-24
surveys of disability, 22, 23-24, 26-27; Health Examination, 23; Health Interview, 22; National Health, 35; Social Security Administration (1966, 1972), 36-38, 48

temporary disability insurance programs (compared to Social Security Disability Insurance), 123-24
Tilton, Timothy, 8
Titmuss, Richard, 7, 11-12

unemployment: disability, 118-19; insurance, 9

values: anti-collectivism, 8; Connally, William, 7; disability insurance, 54-67, 124, 126-27; Furniss, Norman, 7-8; George, Vic (and Wilding, Paul), 7; individualism, 7; Myrdal, Gunnar, 8; Navarro, Vicente, 7; Rein, Martin, 7; Reisman, David, 7; reluctant collectivists, 8, 50, 52, 66-67;

Titmuss, Richard, 7, 11-12; social problem definition, 6-10, 126-27; Social Security Act (1935), 51-54; Weber, Max, 7
Veteran's Administration, 116; benefits (compared to Social Security Disability Insurance), 123
Vietnam War, 15-16

Wagner, Robert F., 56-57
Weber, Max, 7
workers' compensation (compared to Social Security Disability Insurance), 123-24; Temporary Disability Insurance, 116
World War II, 11-12
Wright, Deil, 103

ABOUT THE AUTHORS

IRVING HOWARDS is a professor of political science at the University of Massachusetts, Amherst, Massachusetts.

Dr. Howards has published extensively in the area of public policy analysis of state and local governments in the United States. He recently served as a research professor at the Institute for Research on Poverty of the University of Wisconsin, Madison, Wisconsin. His most recent publication (with Henry Brehm) is, "The Impossible Dream: The Nationalization of Welfare: A Look at Disability Insurance and State Influence over the Federal Government," (*Polity*, Fall, 1978).

Dr. Howards holds a B.A., M.A., and Ph.D. from the University of Wisconsin, Madison, Wisconsin.

HENRY P. BREHM is adjunct associate professor of sociology at the University of Maryland, Baltimore County. He has been affiliated with the University since 1969.

Dr. Brehm has authored and co-authored a series of journal articles and other presentations in the field of sociology. He is a co-author of two books, *Disease, the Individual, and Society* and *Preventive Health Care for Adults*.

Dr. Brehm holds a B.A. and M.A. from New York University and a Ph.D. from the University of Maryland, College Park.

SAAD Z. NAGI is Mershon professor of sociology and public policy at Ohio State University. He has served on several advisory committees on research and demonstration grants in the federal government. Dr. Nagi has been a Fulbright Fellow (1953-55), and was the recipient of the National Rehabilitation Association Award for outstanding contributions through research on disability. His contributions to the research literature in sociology and the health fields include the following books, *Disability and Rehabilitation: Legal, Clinical, and Self-Concepts and Measurement, The Social Contexts of Research,* and *Child Maltreatment in the United States.*

HV   Howards, Irving.
3001
A4H68 Disability, from
        social problem to
        federal program

DATE			
FEB 2			
JUL 6 1984			
MAY 26 1986			
MY 1 '96 MAY 0 1 1999			